**Mike G. Williams**

# Turkey Soup
# for the
# Sarcastic
# Soul

Finding God in the simple, stupid,
and sarcastic moments of life

## Other Books from the Mind of Mike G. Williams

*More Turkey Soup For The Sarcastic Soul* 2003

*Life Happens! Shut Up, Smile, And Carry A Plunger* 2005

*Men are from Mars Because Women Killed the Ones on Venus* 2007

**Please see all of the mike Williams Book, CD, and DVD resources at**

**www.christiancomedian.com**

All scripture references are paraphrased for ease of understanding. And we saved on copyright expenditures!

# Contents

*Dedicated to my wife, Terica, and our son, Chapman*

A special thanks to, my Parents, Phyllis Roddenberry, Steve Smith, Jack Peters, David Burton, Doug Couch, John Garner, Ken Lash, Mark Lowry, Mike Warnke, Justin Fennell, David Letterman, Carrot Top, Conan O'brien, Ken Davis, Tim Jones, Dennis Miller, George Carlin, TJ Foltz, the Great Wall, Compassion International, David Owen, Craig Timmer, New Missions, Tim DeTellis, Danny deArmas, Janet Parshall, Franklin Graham, Bill Gaither, James Dobson, Rosie Greer, Frank Peretti, Duffy Robbins, Mike Singletary, Susie Shellenberger, Cal Thomas, Max Lucado, Charles Swindol, Sheila Walsh, Chuck Colson, Jay Leno, Barry Maguire, Phil Keaggy, Bruce Carroll, Mike Atkinson, Lori Polich, Luciano Pavarotti, Jack Hayford, and to you. A very special thanks to my mentor and friend Ken Davis for his encouragement and help in making this book a reality.

*All praise and honor goes to the King of Kings.*

> I think I need to get my hindsight checked out. Seriously, even when I'm in the shower, I can't see a thing back there.
> *Mike G. Williams*

# Introduction

*I*n 1982, I spent the summer wandering the paths of Nepal, Turkey, Jordan, and Muncie, Indiana, with a great teacher. This wise teacher shared with me some deeply profound concepts along that journey. These were truly days of great spiritual awakening for me. Of course, none of them are included in this book. Do you really think I would sell deeply profound concepts for fourteen bucks? You have got to be kidding.

This book actually started sixteen years ago. I was a newly wedded man with a seventeen-second attention span with a wife committed to seeing her husband become the spiritual head of the home. My personal devotional life at that time was all but non-existent, and my desire to spend time reading was quickly thwarted by whatever was offered on ESPN. Reading at all was reduced to whatever book or magazine was lying on the back of the toilet. My wife found that by putting a daily devotional guide like *Our Daily Bread* in the un-mentionable place, by sheer habit I would get a spiritual start on the day (and often a spiritual finish, too).

Over the past sixteen years, I have shared the proverbial water closet with Oswald Chambers, Max Lacado, Charles Swindoll, Mike Yaconelli, Billy Graham, Stuart Smalley, Ken Davis, and many other fine Christian authors. We even noticed that a good case of the flu could generate a spiritual revival in my life.

For some time now, I have had a desire to write a book for people like myself who have difficulty finding any time for a daily devotional. I wanted to title it *My First Bathroom Reader* or *My Constitutional-Devotional*. The book would come complete with a Velcro leg strap and would include a study of the Gospel of John. *Please pardon the pun.* I'm sure the publisher will not let me do that, so I doubt that any of you are actually reading this. Then there was *Chicken Soup for the Porcelain Bowl.* Unfortunately, the good folks at the Chicken Soup Publishing conglomerate already own the phrase, Chicken Soup for the... *Everything!*

So, after much contemplation and introspection I have settled on a compromise. I welcome you to *Turkey Soup for the Sarcastic Soul!* You will find a few jokes to make you laugh, a few honest thoughts from a warped mind, and a little help in finding God in the simple and stupid things of life. On a positive note, our Turkey contains no *Tryptophan,* so you won't be nodding off during the read!

Be aware that the jokes contained within these pages have been compiled over the past ten years. The ones I did not personally write were written down as I remember hearing them, so they may not be verbatim. I have also been known to forget distasteful adjectives and adverbs from time to time. I have attempted to give credit to the person I heard use it first. However, there are no guarantees of authenticity expressed or implied.

Due to my acute attention deficit disorder, I tend to jump from one random thought to another. This may require you the reader to pay close attention to the intended subject for me while I attempt to reconnect my frontal lobe.

Mike G. Williams

# Right Arm, Left Arm, Right Foot, Head Back

*It's always darkest before dawn. So if you're going to steal your neighbor's newspaper, that's the time to do it.*

Justin Fennell

*I*t was in the country of Haiti where I saw a sight that I will never forget. It was not the sight of the beautiful sun-drenched beaches, nor was it the houses made of sticks. It was not the faces of the little children that held up their hands for a piece of candy. It was not the little Toyota truck taxis that they pile twenty people into and onto. Burned into my memory is a wrinkled old man who led the children.

I was down there on a trip to New Missions. They are a wonderful child relief agency that really makes a difference in the lives of five thousand children every day. A group of friends had joined me to go and be the great white saviors of Haiti with our guitars and bags of candy. Little did we know how little we knew. Arrogance is an American tradition at times.

> Have you ever groped blindly through the middle of a packed suitcase trying to find something and then you suddenly realize with horror that your razor blades had come unwrapped? Me too.
> *George Carlin*

It was in a little village, in a tiny one-room school, where I saw the little teacher, leading songs from Sunday school. He led them in a prayer and sang the B.I.B.L.E. That is when I noticed that he only had one knee. *Sorry for the poetry.* If I had not been standing to the side, I never would have known he was missing a leg. He then went on to lead the students in the singing of *Father Abraham.* You know the song. It pretty much engages every appendage of the body. I watched to see what he would do. He sang, "right arm, left arm, right leg, head back." I wanted to yell out, "Hey stop, you missed the left leg," but I didn't. They skipped right over the left leg as if it wasn't even there. Well, I guess in his case, it wasn't. The children had learned the song from him and did not know the song included the swinging of a left leg. The old man didn't seem to miss that line either. He had the joy. He knew the strength. I'll never forget that man.

Margaret was going blind. Upon learning of her impending condition, she contacted her sister Patricia for some consolation. Her sister listened intently, mourned at the appropriate spots, and prayed earnestly. A few days later at the local drug store, Patricia, who had always been a bit of a prankster, sent her soon-to-be-blind sister a beautifully crafted card. She also sent a cheap tin cup and handful of pencils. What a cruel joke. What impervious insensitivity! When the ailing sister received the card and the moronic gift, she was then faced with a few optional responses. She could get angry at her sister's insensitivity and fire back a bitter response. She could get angry with

God. She could cry out in justifiable grief over the loss of her precious sight. Or, she could cling to the humor of the gift, the gift of the humor, even though it may seem crass to you and me. What do you think she did? You're right, I'm not going to give you a bad example. *That would be pretty stupid of me.* Over the next few years, she traveled the country with her tin cup and pencils and shared how laughter can change any situation. She had the joy. She knew the strength. She chose to live in the joy rather than the obvious. Strange concept.

Erik Weihenmayer was the first blind man to climb Mt. Everest. I watched this articulate spokesman describe his climb on the television news. I do not remember the entire interview, but I do remember one thing that really slapped me in the face. He laughed and said, "People have been afraid to use the word blind in my presence, like I'm going to hear the word blind and start thinking about my blindness and start crying. Blindness is not really like a huge barrier. It's just really kind of something that's an inconvenience. Sometimes it makes your life more complicated, and sometimes it makes things take a bit longer. But it just doesn't have to be the block or the wall." Hmmm, I think Eric has seen something that can't be seen! I believe that he may have the joy!

> Scientists tell us that if you took the average man's intestines and laid them out end to end... Man, would that hurt.
>
> *Tim Jones*

When Ezra had read the Law of Moses to the people, they wept. I would like to think it was from guilt. The Law always shows us our shortcomings. A little guilt is good for us from time to time. It causes us to re-examine our lives. Nehemiah and Ezra said to the people, "This day is holy unto God, eat and drink and give to those who have nothing, and do not be grieved, for the joy of the Lord is your strength." And as I sit here today, it would be easy for me to bask in the guilt of my past mistakes. Nevertheless, I too will take the wine and the bread in reverent celebration. I will partake of the body and blood of Christ. I will receive forgiveness of sins. Great joy can now overflow my soul as I arise from the table clean. It will be my strength for the day, and from that strength, I will give to those in need.

> I used to think that I could jump off the top of the roof and fly. I never really got up the nerve to really try it. Especially when my cat kept failing at it over and over again. I miss that cat.
>
> *Mike G. Williams*

The scriptures did *not* say that my strength would be a joy to me. Rather, they say that the joy of the Lord would be my strength. This is not a matter of semantics. When you have the joy, it gives you strength to face the situations. I want to challenge you to immerse yourself in the joy of God. Let His grace and mercy flow over you through the table of communion. Count your blessings. Name them one by one. Make a big fat list of the good things. Write them down and pin them to your desk. Share them with a friend or even a stranger. Sing a new song to the Lord. Write it yourself. Then watch as you gain strength to deal with your circumstances. I know it will. I guarantee it! *Better than Ezra!*

**Prayer:** *God of great power and love, I come to You now. I ask that Your joy permeate my heart. I ask that this joy go deep into my soul and become for me a well of strength. May I be a source of inspiration for others today through the way I handle my life. Amen.*

*Do not be grieved for the joy of the Lord is your strength.*
Nehemiah 8:10

# 2

# I Have a
# No Nudity Policy

*Ever notice how every time Sally Strothers comes on T.V. for Feed the Children she's a little bit bigger? Hey, Sally, it's Feed the Children, not Eat the Children.*

Mike G. Williams

Okay, possibly the most embarrassing day of my life befell me last year in the Dominican Republic. I was flying in one of those little forty passenger CRJ's. A *Canadair Regional Jet* is the official name. I was sicker than a dog from brushing my teeth with the tap water in Santo Domingo. No, we Americans shouldn't even do that. I was not alone in my sickness, although in my opinion, I was in the worst condition. The flight was not extremely long, but it was too long for me, if you know what I mean. Now, I am a big boy of almost six-two and I weigh in at a muscular two-twenty. *Canadian!*

*Whatever!* The CRJ has a lavatory that was designed by dwarf elves and specially built by vertically challenged anorexics on a forty-day fast. I entered that sardine can rather hurriedly, only to find that I could not get my pants down while facing the door. There was no room to bend! *Some of you big guys can sympathize with me.* So I turned around using the room above the commode to bend my body forward in a way that would allow me to drop the proverbial trousers and then turn back around. If this is getting too graphic for you, please skip to the next chapter. It was at this point that G-forces and metal fatigue fought their final duel and metal fatigue lost. The door of that tiny lavatory shot open from the weight of my backside. *I hate it when that happens!*

> I bet if one of the original thirteen colonies had been a nudist colony, the British would not have been so quick to fire on them. Because, hey, what kind of creep is going to shoot at a naked guy!
>
> *Tim Jones*

Fortunately, the flight attendant was on the blind side of the door. The other thirty-eight short-term missionaries were not so lucky. They had no idea their trip to the Dominican included a lunar eclipse. Someone later commented about the moon being so full that the tides were rising.

All of my pride was now gone. *You could say that it flew out the door.* My name was changed from Rev. Williams to Rev. Sum Big Moon! It was what ministers

> A man in Waldo, Florida shot himself in the buttocks while putting on his pants. Then he had a neighboor pour gunpowder in the wound and light it as a disinfectant.
>
> Later, at the hospital, he said, "It just seemed like a good idea at the time."
>
> *From a Newspaper Article*

later call a deeply moving, spiritually enlightening experience, but not at that moment. Surprisingly, for the next six days, I could lead the devotions for this group without any pretense.

They had seen me at my worst. For the first time in my teaching career, I could be totally honest.

Now, I am not advocating nudity in any form. Coming from a conservative Baptist background, I even frown on it between married couples. *It could lead to dancing!* I am saying that we need to be real with each other. Let's put aside our Calvins and our Hillfigers and realize that we are all just strangers and vagabonds trying to find our way home. Our ability to really make a difference in people's lives has not been because of how perfect we are, but rather because of how real we have been. It is our ability to show brokenness and God's ability to fix brokenness that has allowed us to have an impact on people.

Jesus fed more than five thousand people with five loaves of bread and two little fishes. My wife often reminds me that it was not merely a prayer that multiplied the food. It was when Jesus blessed it and *broke it* that it fed the masses. Wow, broken bread fed the multitude. Just like a broken body fed the world. God uses breakable, broken, and formerly broken things. It is His specialty.

**Prayer:** *Great Father who sent Jesus into a broken world, to be broken for it, break me. May I demonstrate Your ability to heal the hurts and comfort the downhearted by allowing Your work in me to be revealed. May my life represent the hospital where the sick come to be mended. Amen.*

*Taking the five loaves and two fish, He looked up to heaven, and blessed and broke the loaves, more than five thousand people were fed and of the broken pieces leftover were enough to fill twelve baskets full.*
Matthew 14:19-21

**3**

# Forget About the
# Weather Already

*Do not walk behind me, for I may not lead.*
*Do not walk ahead of me, for I may not follow.*
*Do not walk beside me, either; just leave me alone.*

Justin Fennell

*W*hen I'm home my radio is most often set to FM 91 WKES in Lakeland, Florida. Many years ago I did comedy writing and voice-overs for the FM 91 morning show. It was under different ownership then and I really enjoyed my time there until I got fired. *Sure, I'll tell you why.* One of my humorous characters was known as Michael G. Williams, President of Former Elvis Impersonator Ministries. Once a week, I would have a jelly donut chat and give encouragement to Elvis impersonators who were trying to get free of that lifestyle. It was basically recycled old Elvis jokes with the closing tag line, "Elvis is dead, now put that peanut butter and 'nana sandwich down, get off the couch, take off the cape, and get on with your life!" Now you can understand why I was fired.

Each week the phone lines would light up with people calling in to voice their opinion about our comedy sketches. Many called in to give us high praise for being on the cutting edge of Christian Radio. Alas, one week there was one caller who felt that we had taken the

> I disagree with unanimity.
> *Mike Atkinson*

fun over the legal limit, and he would not be supporting the station anymore. Did you say no support money? Enough said! Michael G. the Elvis character was now officially dead. *Well, dead again depending on whether or not you believe he was dead in the first place.* The owners had made the decision and my career as a morning radio guy was over in one jelly doughnut-induced moment. But, that was then and this is now. *I'm not bitter!*

I love the new station owners and the Moody programming is excellent. The announcers are genuinely nice people. Ruth Dinwiddie is the afternoon host and makes everyone feel as if [Mom] was on the air. Ruth is sincerely a wonderful lady who knows a little about what it's like to be scrutinized by the public, so my sarcastic jest will not surprise her in any way. Ruth is infatuated with the weather! She comes on every afternoon multiple times and says, "It's 85 in Lakeland, 85 in Orlando, 84 in Tampa, 85 in Seffner, 84 in Sarasota, 84 in Bradenton, 83 in St. Petersburg, 84 in Brandon, 86 in Clearwater, and at the Tampa International Airport, it is 85 degrees. The 'feels like temperature' is 86 degrees. We have a 50% chance of mid-afternoon showers and the humidity is 84 percent." Who cares! Just say, "It's about 85 outside, get used to it! But really, who cares what the temperature is outside? We are inside, listening to the radio in climate-controlled comfort. If you need to know the temperature, open the door or roll down a window, you lazy sea slug!

I know that there are some shut-ins who can't get to a door or window, but they are not going outside anyway! Why depress them by telling them how beautiful it is out there? Tell them it's a combination monsoon-blizzard out there and they are better off at home in bed. And frankly, who cares about the *feels like* temperature. It is 85 degrees, so who cares if it feels like it is 87 degrees? Work with me, people. And may I ask, is John and Mary Traveler really concerned with the airport temp? Are they really going to postpone a flight to see the grandkids because outside the airport is 2 degrees higher than at their house? No! They have air-conditioning at Tampa International now. Who knew? *They have new things called Jets that are really catching on, too.*

> Okay, I know better now, but if your fiancée ever asks if you would ever leave her, do not say, "Who wants to know?"
> *Tim Jones*

Let's talk about rain and humidity. For your information, we always have a 50% chance of showers in central Florida. You may think we need to know the humidity. After all, people say, "It's not the heat, it's the humidity." No it's not! *It's the spittle fryin' heat!* When it's 50 degrees out, nobody says, "Oh man, the temp is not to high, but mixed with the humidity, I am burning up."

What is the [Mr. Forgetful] listening demographic that requires us to report on the weather every fifteen minutes? I calculated the average time it takes to give the weather and multiplied it by the times it was given. We lose two hours a day to trivial temp changes. *Not to mention the time I lost in figuring out how much time we lose.* We could have four more high quality shows if they would shove the thermometer in the trash. Better yet, stick the thermometer in Ruth's nose and let's ask her the 'feels like' temperature. Give me music. Give me preaching. Give me a prayer time. Death to weather information! *I love you Ruth.*

Let me add that I can understand the giving of hurricane warnings. Please tell me when a tornado is blowing up my alley, but thunderstorms, c'mon! Think about this. When was the last time you came home to find your house wiped out by a thunderstorm? Do we really need special preparation for these? I have never heard my neighbor say, "Oh man, a thunderstorm is coming! I better put a roof on the mobile home before it gets here! Honey, where's the plywood and duct tape?"

It feels good to get that off my chest. It's just that trivial, meaningless information bothers me. *Although, I guess one person's trivia is another person's devotional book. Hmmm.* With as little spare time as we have, the last thing we need to do is fill our lives with trivial information. There is just so little time compared to the task ahead of us. But God gives us all enough time to do everything He asks us to do. Provided we don't waste the time He gives us playing Nintendo 64 or watching The Weather Channel.

What are the unimportant things that are choking the life out of your important things? Take a big black marker and cross them out of your mind. You can do bad things, or you can do good things—or you can do the best things. Don't get rid of bad and settle for good when God wants great. God has given you this day as a gift to use, as you will. He has given you talents to use, as you will. He has given you a calling to use, as you will. So now *will* you?

Make a quick list of the five most important areas of your life. Divide those areas by your non-sleeping and non-working hours, and now you have master plan. *You know that I am both contemplative and introspective.* "In a perfect world," you say. Yes, but it is a start. You may want to list your kids, your spouse, your faith, your sanity time, schooling, time to finish this great book, *and time to order more stuff from my website.*

> There are days when I feel like I have lost the human race.
> *Mike G. Williams*

Remember that whatever we do with our time today, we are exchanging a day of our life for it. That is heavy! I want it to be great and not just good; so that I will not regret the very high price I have paid for it. The days are desperate, so live that way. We must place an awesome premium on our time.

**Prayer:** *Father, in these dangerous times that we live, I pray that I might put my priorities in order. May the investment of time I make today be in service to You and not to frivolous pursuits. Amen.*

*Be careful to live as wise people and make the most of your time. These are desperate days that require us to think and to be careful.*
Ephesians 5:15-16

# A Perfect Place—
# Almost

*My Dad used to put my slip-and-slide on the gravel drive-
way! It taught me that life is fun, though sometimes painful.*

Mike G. Williams

used to live in the lovely city of Chicago. Visit sometime, but stay off the rapidly moving public trans-
portation system known as the L. In my neighborhood, the L
stood for, Last stop before a mugging, Locate a handgun, Let
senior citizens sit before stealing their bags, and Look, that guy
just barfed on my shoe. *Okay, so I got carried away, get over it.*
My biological family comes from the South Side. Some of you
know all of what that means.

I now live on what is called the I-4 corridor. It is that massive chunk of blacktop that runs across Florida from Tampa to

Daytona Beach. The road runs through what is considered to be some of the most prime real estate in the world. It is called Disney World. Have you been to the number one vacation destination in the western hemisphere? Yea, even the galaxy? Anyone? The beautiful tropical landscape and lush green fiberglass forests are hard to beat. The manmade lakes are flood- and drought-proof and filled with friendly lifeguards. If they could just control the weather, it would be like heaven. In fact, so many people have made the statement, "I wish I could just live here," that they have built a city. It's called *Celebration*.

> I don't let my kids stay overnight at anyone's house. That's how Kato Kaelin got started.
> *Taylor Mason*

The sidewalks are swept every night and the lawns are mowed. There is never any trash placed out on the curb. No vagrants on the street corners. No boats in the backyards or cars on blocks out front. No noisy neighbors. It is quite expensive, and you have to fill out an application to live in this magical kingdom, I mean community. Which are two big reasons why I could never live there.

The downtown is a colorful array of shops and boutiques. A retro fashioned movie theater and a Starbucks offer entertainment and refreshment for all. The Bakery makes all the bread products fresh every day, and a hometown grocery store will deliver your canned goods in a few hours. The local downtown hotel offers an extra room overlooking the golf course for your guests. There are wonderful restaurants and a friendly little café. All of which is garbed to look circa 1950. Office space is available right next to a modern full-service hospital disguised to look like another

> When I was a kid, we were so poor that we didn't have water. We would have to suck the liquid out of mud.
> *Dom Irrera*

well-manicured office building. In spite of the vermin on their logo, they have excellent pest and rodent control. What an absolutely perfect place!

I could not help but laugh as I drove in and out of Celebration. The hospital is right next to the welcome sign. Fitting place for a hospital to be, I believe. It could be easy to forget a place like that when you are living in *Walt Pleasantville*. When you are surrounded by pleasantries, it is easy to forget the inevitable. But every time someone comes in or out of this imaginative community, they are reminded of life's fragility. The large white "H" on the reflective blue sign says it all. They can't get away from it. It does not matter how much money they spend on *the stuff*, they cannot escape an appointment with disappointment. None of us can escape the time when the body breaks down and there is no way to fix or replace it.

> If this plane goes down in the frozen tundra, I want you to know I will waste no time starving myself while debating the inevitable. The inevitable, being the moral and ethical issues of cannibalism. Just know the weakest among you will get eaten first.
>
> *Mike G. Williams*

Rumors say that Walt Disney himself is frozen in some cryogenic vault waiting for a *cure for death*. It may be a while. Life reduces the young and the old, the rich and the poor, to a common denominator: disappointment. We have all had hopes and dreams, plans for more. We have all lived as if tomorrow would always come and the bills would not. The inevitable always happens. Disappointment can be one nasty mother-in-law.

As a believer in Christ Jesus, I rest in the great promise that one day the disappointments will pass away. My life has been filled with the D word. It started when I was born and my world did not meet my complete approval. It continued through my teen years, when my parents would not let me have a drum set. I bathed in disappointment during high school when I had to settle for something less than being voted prom king. The college of my choice did not return my calls. The car of my dreams sure wasn't my Ford Pinto. On a serious note, I've seen family problems, cancer, death, incarceration, and reality all around me. I know the D word. So I *must* learn to rest in the fact that though our world is full of disappointments, Jesus has overcome the world. Through that overcoming, He has prepared for us a future that is not even influenced by the disappointment. So hold on my friend, hold on.

**Prayer:** *Father, in this age where disappointment is on every hand, we ask that You would give us peace. Give us the ability to rest in the fact that joy is soon coming. Give us strength to go on and never ever give up. We trust You. Amen.*

*God will wipe away every tear from their eyes and there shall be no more death and no more pain.*
Revelation 21:4

# This Too
# Shall Pass

*An optimist believes a pitcher to be half full. A pessimist says the pitcher is half empty. I say the pitcher is half empty, the water is polluted and the glass is cracked.*

Danny Murphy

*a*s a fat guy, I should not be allowed in the grocery store. I should be stopped at the door! It is like inviting Cheech and Chong to Woodstock. Okay, that was not nice. It is like taking Fat Albert to a pizza buffet. Was that nicer? Of course it was, because overeating is not as big of a sin as drug addiction. Sorry, I forgot. Anyway, I'm reading the labels in the medicine aisle. It's how I pass time when I get dragged to the grocery store. You really should do it sometime. On some children's cough syrups, it warns you not to use it while operating heavy machinery. My four-year-old really loves to hop on the backhoe when he's got pneumonia. An eye drop company warned me to not put eye drops in while driving a car. They are right in saying that. I tried that once and almost dropped my cell phone. A nasal decongestant suggests that I not take the product while scuba diving. There's a *Survivor* challenge waiting to happen. And one laxative motto says, "It Works While You Sleep!" Baby, the last thing I want to do is wake up one morning and find out they were truthful in their advertising. Sorry!

> If you think nobody cares if you're even alive, try missing a couple of house payments.
>
> *Justin Fennell*

I have a tendency to make a mountain out of a molehill. On the other hand, I have been known to trivialize the important things as well. But today is no molehill. Today, I move my mother to a new nursing home so she can be in the same place as my father. I must find time to visit them both and take another family member to counseling (not me this time). I was asked to deal with a disgruntled church member who is threatening to leave the church. I have to write a letter to a T-shirt company who owes me money. Later, I can return twelve urgent phone calls that came while I was outside trying to change a flat tire. You are possibly thinking I made that all up. Well you would be *the weakest link*. Wrong! Are you having one of those days, also? Weeks? Months? How about years?

> I was on Third Street and I had to get to Seventh Street and I was confused as to which way to turn. Then I remembered Einstein postulating that parallel lines eventually meet. They are dredging my car from the lake right now.
>
> *Emo Phillips*

Let me start this paragraph by saying that I promise you this will not be my deepest thought for the week. It is almost too simple. Yet I am so thankful for these simple words repeated over and over in scripture: "and it came to pass." I know you can find a few places where my thoughts might be a little out of context, but work with me for a moment. As I look back over my life, I see that this day of mine is not unique. There have been other days that have been just as emotionally frustrating. There have been days so tragic that we have anniversaries marking them. But they have all passed, only to be replaced by another set.

> When life hands you lemons, you can always make lemonade, and sit on the curb in the hot blazing sun and try to sell that lukewarm lemonade, until some bully comes by, drinks your lemonade, and beats you up.
> *Mike G. Williams*

I want to challenge you to seize the moment. Embrace the day's experiences with gusto. Good, bad, or indifferent, we have twenty-four hours in which to respond to a challenge to live godly lives. Tomorrow will soon be here, leaving today in its wake. What matters most is how we respond to the swill we are somehow asked to walk through. Rejoice in the fact that we do not walk through it alone. I will not quote from *Footprints in the Sand*, although that poem was really touching the first six-hundred times I heard it, but I do know the Creator of the universe stands beside us every day.

Jerry Lewis closes his Labor Day Telethon each year with a Rodgers and Hammerstein classic:

> *When you walk through the storm hold your head up high,*
>     *and don't be afraid of the dark.*
> *At the end of the road is a golden sky, and the sweet silver*
>     *song of the lark.*
> *Walk on through the wind, Walk on through the rain,*
>     *Though your dreams be tossed and blown.*
> *Walk on, Walk on, with hope in your heart, and you'll never*
>     *walk alone, you'll never walk alone!*

I should be an ad writer. I think a better laxative motto would be, "And It Came To Pass." I also believe a better life motto would be, "And It Came To Pass." That is just my personal opinion.

**Prayer:** *God, I desire to meet the challenge of today with spiritual expectancy. I acknowledge that You are in control. I want to keep my eyes on You and wait for Your victory and for Your tomorrow. Help me. Amen.*

*And it came to pass...*
The Bible (too many times to reference)

*Yes, all that live godly in Christ Jesus will suffer.*
2 Timothy 3:12

**6**

# Dragon Tales

*The pen may be mightier than the sword, but I would prefer an Uzi in a gang fight!*

Mike G. Williams

*J*ehoshaphat was in a bad predicament. He had just been warned that the vast armies of Moabites and Ammonites and a few mercenary Meunites were coming to make war on him. We all know how vicious those mercenary Meunites can be. Any king worth his weight in cheese grits would have quickly gathered his generals and prepared for war. At least he would circle the wagons, take the women and children inside, and boil some water. But this king realized that he was outnumbered about seventy-five to one. At this point, the king had a better chance of Ed McMahon and the Prize Patrol dropping by his tent with a check. I personally would have been preparing to negotiate a peaceful settlement and hope that I could get out of town with my family, our tents, our sheep, and our donkeys intact.

> No one is listening until you make a mistake.
> *Justin Fennell*

However, the king decided on another route. He called everyone together and was very open about the problem. During this time in history, kings were not as concerned with re-election possibilities, exit poles, or separation of church and state. He cried out to God, "We have no power to face this vast army that is attacking us. We do not know what to do, but our eyes are on you." What a moron! Didn't he know that God helps those who help themselves? I guess not. Jehoshaphat knew the "G" rule. Do you know that rule? Not the golden one. It says, "Glance at your circumstances and gaze at God." *One more time because repetition is the best teacher.* "Glance at your circumstances and gaze at God." Put the focus on God rather than the problem. Some of you psych people are screaming right now, "You're living in denial!" No! We are living in truth. Take your medications and follow along, doctor.

So, the king marched into an un-winnable war, led by a bagpipe and accordion group. I'm sure the band was glad to be picked for this front-line honor. Keyboard players and guitarists love to risk their fingers in a sword fight. *I would have had the group led by the mimes, because I love mimes and you can't shoot them because they are always in a box!* The singers were instructed in a one-line chorus. They bellowed, "Praise the Lord, for His love and mercy endures forever." I would have had them sing something a little more intimidating like, "Awesome God," or "Mighty Warrior," or "You Better Run Fast, Because Our God Is About To Kick Some Moabite Booty." Do you ever sing that one at your church? It's a little wordy, but the youth like it.

> How can I learn any history? They keep adding new events!
> *Taylor Mason*

The choir sang as they crossed the plain. Strangely, the enemy soldiers, who were ready to spring on their foes, turned and began to fight each other. By the time Jehoshaphat got to the battlefield, it was strewn with dead bodies. Not one enemy had escaped and it took three days for the king to collect the spoilage of war. Apparently, in those days people would bring their finest spoilage, treasures, artwork, and livestock out with them to a good battle. I really don't know exactly why. There could have been a huge crime problem back in their village. But I do know that you need to *glance at your circumstances and gaze at God.*

Here is how this relates to me. I may be the big fish in my little bowl, but compared to all the bowls around me, I am outnumbered seventy-five million to one. My battles today need to be faced honestly. What kind of foe do you face today? Glance at the circumstances and gaze at God. This is possibly the greatest lesson I have learned for dealing with life. It is not easy, but when I have placed my trust in God, I have seen His miraculous hand at work.

**Prayer:** *Father, today I face situations that I cannot overcome in my own strength. Circumstances have become overwhelming. I choose to gaze at You and to thank You for Your steadfast love and tender mercy. I trust You. Help me to trust You more. I will praise You as I wait for Your divine deliverance. Amen.*

*We have no power to face this vast army that is attacking us. We do not know what to do, but our eyes are on You.*
2 Chronicles 20:12

# It's About Winning
# *and* How You
# Play the Game

*I want to participate in Olympic Snoozing. I think I could
medal in that.*

Paula Poundstone

*N*ow, I have never been extremely competitive. Maybe
that's why I do fairly well at golf. I race the cart
around, singing all the old songs, and have a blast. I'm not out
there on the green getting stressed out over a missed shot. I enjoy
the fact that I am not in the office or slumping over a computer
screen yelling, "Think funny, think funny!" Most of my golf days
have been wonderful experiences, with the exception of the day
my #3 wood broke as I swung at the ball. The head flew off and hit
a duck in the back of the neck. I felt really bad for the next three
or four holes. I'm not a member of *PETA*, but I am technically a
minister, so we had a little duck funeral and I said a few words.

There was also the time I forgot to set a parking brake on a golf cart. Courses have insurance for things like that. It's practically expected, even though it had not happened in the ninety-year history of the club. The look on that tennis player's face made the two hundred and fifty dollar deductible worth it.

But, there is one other day I recall. Maybe my medications were out of whack. It was a beautiful day, and everyone but me was playing a personal best. I was having what my friends have since called, "The Bermuda Triangle of my golfing career." On this particular day, I topped every ball and missed every putt. My mulligan was gone at the first tee. My normal slice had become a hook, so I spent more time in the water and the woods than Bill Dance and Orlando Wilson. *Bill and Orlando are outdoor sportsmen, ladies!*

I choked and took a ten on the fourteenth and a nine on the fifteenth and sixteenth. I survived seventeen with an eight and faced the final horizon. This was my last opportunity to prove that I was actually *just toying* with them on the previous seventeen holes. I can remember someone quoting a line from *Casey at Bat* as I adjusted my grip. I spouted in resolution, "Gentleman, if *this* ball does not get off the tee, I will see that the club does!" That's how my driver came to be in a hovering position almost a hundred feet above the ground. That's how my club got lodged in the top of a tree. That's how four guys came to be seen climbing a tree. That's how you get asked to leave a course. That's a shame too. I really miss *that* club.

We are called to play a game of life today. It will be on the concrete greens of corporate America, the tough courses of the factory, the backyards of our homes, and they will all be very public courses. We will have our swings scrutinized by the players

> I would like to see Olympic Sumo wrestling sponsored by a diaper manufacturer. The visual would only confirm what everybody has been thinking for years. "That last match brought to you by Pampers Ultimate—they now hold up to 500 pounds."
>
> *Mike G. Williams*

around us, as if they have a right. We have to play on, even though we can't clearly see the flag. The course can seem very unforgiving at times. We are asked to lovingly play through the others who would bog the course with apathy. We are asked to

> It's a dangerous thing to hold the Olympics in Atlanta. You know when they let the doves lose some good old boy is going to pull out a shotgun and start blasting.
>
> *Jeff Foxworthy*

play on through the days of discouragement. We are asked to repair our damaged greens for the ones who are coming after us. Sometimes tragedy strikes like lightning, and we don't get to finish our round. We are asked to play for our lives, live at peace with our fellow man, and enjoy the game. Sure, no problem!

Let me break it down to these few words. First of all, be encouraged, because you have been called and chosen to play in the game. Secondly, choose a godly partner. It can be a long cart ride with a partner who has no concept of the sport. Thirdly, play the game with people who are on the same course as you. Fourthly, remember that your alliances will determine the speed of your game. Fifthly, play each hole as if it alone determines the victory. Lastly, remember that every stroke represents a family member, a friend, a neighbor, a job, a church, or a mission. Together, they make up the entirety of the game.

**Prayer:** *Dear Lord, may I participate in life to its fullest. May I realize the gravity of every decision and the far-reaching effect of my choices. May I keep my eyes on the goal every moment of every day. Amen.*

*Let us run the race of life with perseverance, looking unto Jesus, the author and finisher of our faith, who for the prize set before Him endured the cross.*
Hebrews 12:1-2

# 8

# A Chicken
# in Every Pot?

*Our two-party political system is splintered worse than a
jammed door at Chuck Norris's house.*

Dennis Miller

To be honest with you, when I go into the voting booth, I simply try to vote for whomever I think is going to be the lesser of two evils. I often say, "Pick the least worst!" Lately, our choices have been limited to Moe, Larry, or Curly, with an occasional write-in vote for Shemp. I live in Florida, and I never want to hear the words "dangling chad," "dimples," or "recount" again. I never want a president to have to appear on national television and lie to me about an affair. Let's limit the lying to political issues, like fund raising or pardons. As a comedian, I was ready to give Clinton another four years, for a total of twelve. Good or bad, he provided me with more hours of foolish fodder than any successor could possibly hope to deliver.

Next time the election rolls around, I want to see a change in the issues! Let the next big "hot potato" issue be *Hammer Control.* Did you know that more people are hit in the head with a hammer each year than are shot with a gun? *That is no joke, Bob Vila!* We need tighter tool regulations. I think we need hardware stores to instigate background checks, three-day waiting periods, the works. Seriously, building a birdhouse can wait three days. I also want lawn care legislation. It will disallow my neighbor to mow his lawn when I am having dinner on the back porch. There are times when I think that he waits until we get the food on the table and then he runs out and removes all the mufflers from his gas-powered lawn tools, brings them to the edge of his yard and fires them up simultaneously! He continues to run them and rrrrr-rev them until our dinner time is over, and we go back into the house. We have to shout the dinner prayer, just so God can hear it. I have been so angry with him that I have almost attacked him with a weed-eater. *You thought I would say hammer, didn't you?*

I have a confession. Here it goes. I have spent *countless hours* being critical of our political

> George W. Bush is going to visit the Pope. The Pope said he was excited to meet an American President who believed all of the Ten Commandments.
> *Jay Leno*

> It's unbelievable how government programs work in synchronicity. For example, here are two government programs with the same definition: WELFARE = giving money and expecting nothing in return. CAMPAIGN CONTRIBUTION = giving money and...
> *Taylor Mason*

leaders and *countable minutes* praying for them. I should be flogged. *Which, by the way, is still legal in Mississippi.* I have written hundreds of jokes making fun of our leaders and never written a prayer. If our leaders are really ordained by the Lord, then

> If it is really true that the show is over when the fat lady sings, how come we don't go home after the first karaoke song?
> *Mike G. Williams*

maybe there is a master plan to what God is doing through them. Quite possibly, if we were viewing this whole thing from a loftier perch, we would see a rhyme and reason. I wholeheartedly endorse the candidates that represent godly views while remembering that God may choose to take things in a different direction. He has a master plan, and I must trust Him. There are times when God causes calamity to fall on a nation to help them turn towards Him.

I want to challenge you to join me in the following commitment. Every time I tell a politically motivated joke, *and I will*, I will also whisper a prayer along with it. Admittedly, I have not stated that I will tell no more political jokes. Rather, I will attempt to balance the scales with a prayer, too. It may not be full revival, but it is a start. Will you join me?

**Prayer:** *Father, please guide our leaders. Force their hand to righteousness. May our nation and the nations around the world return to You in such a way that Christian leaders will be the natural outpouring of our votes. May we all live lives worthy of our calling. Amen.*

*Let everyone be subject to the governing authorities for God has instituted the governing authorities that exist.*
Romans 13:1

# 9

# Never Bother an
# Agitated Alligator

*Always drink upstream from the herd and never squat with your spurs on.*

Will Rogers

*J* was driving my little white pickup back from teaching a Bible study. *I wouldn't have had to mention the Bible study to make the story, but I like to seem as spiritual as possible.* It was a fairly busy road, and I was clipping along at a good pace, when I saw it on the side of the road! A seven-foot alligator! He or she, *I can't tell the difference in alligators,* was trying to cross the traffic in the dark. I imagine his little pond had dried up from the drought and there were a few moist ones on the other side of the road. His mouth was open wide as he hissed at the cars buzzing past. Most of the four-wheeled motorists did not even see the dark green form at the shoulder of the road. I made a quick U-turn and turned my hazard lights on. I grabbed my flashlight and jumped out of the truck.

Now, I live here, and I have seen these prehistoric predators many times at the lakes and rivers. I have a picture of me wrestling a fiberglass one at the Florida Welcome Center. That somehow makes me an expert.

Please stand back, mortals, and watch Mike (*the Alligator Hunter*) Williams help this meat-eater across the road! It has always been my nature to help animals. I wanted to be a veterinarian when I was young. So, I walked up right next to the gator and said, "Easy boy, I'll get you across the road." What a calming voice I must have to match my dim wit. *I am not the sharpest knife in the drawer.* The lunacy of this is that I was now standing toe to toe with an agitated alligator in the dark. I stopped the traffic and went back to walk the alligator across the street. At this point, the long green carnivore had to be thinking that I might be a tasty little Boy Scout snack.

> When preparing for dinner guests, remove all mouse traps from your kitchen and dining areas. Nothing can stop a conversation like a loud snap followed by the high pitched moanful wail of a dying rodent. If this social nightmare occurs, do not show the furry little victim to the guests, unless they first request a viewing.
>
> *Mike G. Williams*

Have you ever had something dawn on you? Good, so you will understand that the reality of the situation was made very clear in a moment, in the twinkling of a reptile's eye. The witnesses say that I jumped about five feet into the air and levitated backwards. Maybe it was the quick motion from his head coming in my direction. Maybe it was the look in his eye. Maybe it was Memphis! But the leap felt right. *Obviously I survived, but I sing Father Abraham differently now.*

> The early bird gets the worm, but the late cat gets the plumper bird.
>
> *Dave Hopping*

It's not safe to be the savior of people either. Ask Jesus! I take a cautious attitude about many things that I view every day. I don't run toward the gunfire anymore. I don't rush into domestic disputes. I learned that from watching *Top Cops*. People can be worse than alligators at times.

Amos gives us a very quick view into the heart of a shepherd. In it, a lamb is caught in the jaws of a lion. Let's be honest, it's over for the lamb. We say keep the herd protected and out of the lion's grasp, but once it happens, go back to the other savable sheep. In contrast, the shepherd's heart rushes in and grabs a hold on the lamb's leg. He pulls and pulls. Pulls so hard that he pulls the leg off the lamb. I would say, "Walk away dude, it's over," but the shepherd goes back in and grabs another leg. "Hello, Mr. Shepherd, that's a lion you're taking food from, think about this." He pulls until he has taken another leg back from the lion's mouth. Some of you may be thinking that he must have been one stupid shepherd. Whether he winds up walking away with two legs or a piece of an ear, God calls it a rescue. Why? Because the shepherd did all that he could.

> Never give up on a stupid idea simply because it is bad and doesn't work. Cling to it even when it is hopeless. Anyone can cut and run, but it takes a very special person to stay with something that is stupid and harmful.
>
> *George Carlin*

It is so much safer to stay on my side of the fence. It is easier to turn my head and say that I don't have the time to get involved because I travel all the time. People really need someone who will be there for them long-term. I can find some pretty creative ways to avoid contact with the sheep. Not to mention my "under the radar principle." Did I tell you that one? I don't mess in Satan's work and he won't mess with mine. *It's win-win. Covey would love it!* The truth is that you and I have been called to be shepherds and rescuers of our children, of our spouses, of our neighbors, and of our world. We have been called to march in where angels fear to tread and get our hands dirty. We are called to have a shepherd's heart.

That gator made it to the other side of the road. God provided a long tree branch, and I learned a great lesson that night. It was confirmed to me that I like gator best with a side order of fries and hush puppies and a big glass of iced tea!

**Prayer:** *Today, Father, I ask that You give me the opportunity to be a rescuer. I don't know what degree of rescue I can handle, but I trust Your judgment of my abilities. I guess You know what You gave me. So today I will take what comes as coming from heaven, and respond as a shepherd should. Amen.*

*The shepherd rescues from the mouth of the lion two legs, or a piece of an ear.*
Amos 3:12

# 10

# Let the
# Spanking Begin

*I had a dream that I died and went to the bad place where
they cut off my arms and legs and I had to spend eternity
working as a Pez dispenser.*

Emo Phillips

**R**eport card days were the worst of times at my
house. The ride home on the bus was filled with
guilt and anguish, especially when the house came into sight.
Once inside the house, I would make up stories as to why my
class didn't get their report cards. All the while knowing that
they had to be signed and returned in three days. So on the
third day of mental torment, I would come in from school and
head straight for the bathroom. Pretending to be very sick, I
would sit there on the commode hoping that my sickness
would birth parental sympathy. Mom would yell through the

door for the report card, and I would shyly slide the card under the door. What happened in the next few minutes is hard to describe. Remember, I couldn't see, because I was locked safely in the bathroom. I could hear them, though: "Oh, Michael. What in the world were you thinking? An F—in creative writing? Did you even try? Are you on drugs?" These and other various phrases came wafting under my door. I left out a few of them so as to not take us all

> Charles Dickens said, "It was the best of times, it was the worst of times." Dickens had multiple personality disorder. Make up your mind Charlie!
> *Mike G. Williams*

for a trip down parental *baggage* lane. You can thank me later!

It was the best of times. It was the worst of times. Dickens could have been describing a scene from the book of Revelation when he wrote those memorable words. Here we have the beloved disciple John exiled to an island, a deserted rock in the Aegean Sea. What a miserable place to be. There are no luxury accommodations; heck, there is not even a Motel Six. *There is nobody to leave the light on for him.* It is truly the worst of times. But then John has a supernatural experience, a spiritual experience. John has a vision of heaven and a glimpse into what awaits on the other side. In spite of his physical condition, he says in the fourth chapter of Revelation that he is *in the Spirit.* Wow, in what better place could one be? He then has a great vision that is anchored in faith. He is blessed with a glimpse into the throne room of God. *There in heaven stood a throne with One seated on*

> The length of a film should be directly related to the endurance of the human bladder.
> *Alfred Hitchcock*

*the throne.* The great question of the ages is answered. Is somebody in charge? Yes. Yes. Yes! Every sunrise, every sunset screams with all of creation, yes.

From that foundation, we have the ability to come out of our secure sanctuaries and face life head-on. We can throw open the windows of our lives and of our souls and shout, "There is a throne and our God is sitting on it! This life is not just mundane trivialities; no longer will I simply occupy space until I die! This day has cosmic eternal purpose! Rejoice!"

> The "Leaning Tower of Pisa" is a lot like life; you gotta take the good with the bad. It's easy to sweep the floors, but you can't play ping-pong or billiards.
>
> *Taylor Mason*

I want to challenge you to allow your sixth sense, your spiritual sense, to transport you for just a moment from the place in which you are now sitting to a throne room. Allow God to reveal Himself to you right now. See Him on His throne as the righteous King of kings and Lord of lords. Rejoice because that Royalty is your *heavenly* Father. Rejoice because there will be no task too big for you to complete and no burden too great for you to bear before the Father calls for the sound of the trumpet. It will then be time for the reunion. That's His promise. You may be trying to figure out what the report card story has to do with this. Well, when I started thinking about this, it all made sense, but now I have no idea.

**Prayer:** *Our Heavenly Father, the God who occupies the throne, be merciful to me today. Give me the strength to complete the tasks set before me with grace. May I not lose sight of the fact that You are ultimately in control. Amen.*

*In the Spirit, I saw an open door, and a throne in Heaven!*
Revelation 4:1-2

# It's Like Following a Map to a Place that Does Not Exist

*Follow your dream! Unless it's the one where you're at work in your underwear during a fire drill.*

Mike Atkinson

*H*ave you rented a car from Hertz lately? For only six additional dollars you get an amazing little onboard computer. It is a full-color, dash-mounted GPS. A Global Positioning Systems satellite something or other, I forget right now. You type in your destination, which is very hard to do while driving through rush hour traffic. In fact, you have to lie to the machine to do that. Yes, lie to the machine. You have to affirm that you are a passenger operating this device if the car is in gear. I'm a driving liar! But I don't think it's a sin to lie to an inanimate object. I mean it's not like I'm swapping computer software or using *Napster*.

I was running a little late, thanks to my air carrier of choice. I grabbed my luggage and headed off to find parking slip H137. In less than five minutes, I was slinked back into my Ford Taurus rental. I typed in my destination and heard a soothing lady's voice come from the machine: "Proceed north for thirty-seven miles." Oh, how great it was to have technology riding in the car with me. If I got lonely, I could scroll through the *Neverlost system* and hear a comforting voice at any time on my journey. I could check out the food and lodging options at the next exit. I could even locate a hospital in case I needed an emergency appendectomy. I was the king of the world!

> Kids don't need a lot of expensive toys to keep them busy. A simple afternoon with your Grandpa's old shotgun and a barn full of cats is loads of fun.
>
> *Mike Williams*

There was a little glitch though. Glitch is a word we use in the South. It means, oops, wait, uh-oh, hmmm, or hey? I stopped at the trucker's plaza for a quick cup of coffee, and when I got back in the car, the computer screen illuminated a question. "Do you want to continue the designated trip?" Yes, enter, yes I am the passenger, enter, enter, enter, enter. I am not the most patient man in the world. My little guide and I then headed down the road together. "Proceed to the hi-lighted route, right turn ahead in two-hundred feet," my microchip angel would say and I followed. Heck, Blind Bartimeus and Stevie Wonder could have driven with this machine. I mentioned that glitch. It seems that I never actually told the GPS system that *my destination* was the designated trip. When I got back in the car I affirmed the designated trip for the renter before me, who was going in my general direction, if you consider *leaving the airport* as a general direction.

> I would explain it to you, but your brain would explode.
>
> *Steven Wright*

I knew something was wrong when I saw the sign that said, "Welcome to Missouri, the Show-Me State." *I guess we're not in Kansas anymore!* I can be a real idiot at times. Usually those times are limited to my waking hours. So I am not a complete and total idiot. I put life on autopilot from time to time.

We have all heard that old story about the guy who put his motor home on cruise control and went back to make a sandwich. Well the story is fiction but the example is non-fiction. Where is your mental GPS taking you today? Are you going where you really want to go? Or are you just

> Do not meddle in the affairs of cannibals— because you are edible and taste good with soy sauce.
>
> *Mike G. Williams*

following in somebody else's lane? Maybe you are going to a state you really don't want to visit.

Be careful to check your map today. Make sure that you are on the designated path that brings you to your intended destination. The Word of God is a great map for life. That is especially true if your destination is peace in life, reason for living, success, joy, and ultimately, heaven. All too often, in our haste to get somewhere, anywhere, we will apathetically follow someone else's journey guide. Have you committed to spending time in the Bible each day? If you don't, you could wind up in the wrong state. Usually that state is *confusion*. There is a treasure at the end of this narrow road we travel, and for that reason, we must keep a close watch on the old compass.

**Prayer:** *Lord, show me today where I have strayed from Your paths. Correct my settings. Help me to find the true north for my life. May I treasure Your Word as a sacred map. Thank You for the scenic paths You take me down and for the super-highways that move me along faster than I thought I was ready to go. Amen.*

*Thy Word is a lamp unto my feet and a light unto my path.*
Psalms 119:105

# 12

# The Big
# Stinking Camper

*Eat one live toad the first thing in the morning and nothing worse will happen to you the rest of the day.*

Mike Atkinson

*I*t was big, very big. Forty feet of aluminum and fiberglass over six chrome wheels. Two air conditioners, a walk-in closet, and a full kitchen with a microwave. It slept eight people comfortably. This was no camper. It was the Trump Towers on Firestone tires! *Sorry, no Firestone joke available at this time.* The cost was just a few thousand more than my lakefront home. *I don't live on a lakefront, but it sounded like a good descriptive phrase.* This was not camping, folks; this was towable luxury. Ironically, it was called the *Wilderness* model. Wilderness, ya, sure!

Do you like to go camping? My family loves to camp. We take out the Sir Edmond Hillary six-man Mountaineer Special every spring for our trek to the forest. We thought *we* were extravagant when we bought a porta-potty so my wife would not have to walk the snake-filled path after dark. It always amazes me how we Americans will spend hundreds of thousands of dollars on huge homes only to spend every spare weekend in an eight-by-eight square of canvas and nylon.

> I hate it when I ask someone a yes or no question and they respond with, "Hey, is the Pope Catholic?" Because I think the Pope's religious views are nobody's business but his own.
> *Tim Jones*

Last year I was invited to speak at an amazing event called Creation Fest. It is sixty-five thousand of your closest friends worshipping and camping together in the mountains of Pennsylvania. When I arrived, I could not help but compare it to the Israelites wandering in the wilderness for forty years. The exception is that it only lasts a week and that Creation Fest founder, Harry Thomas, has procured a few hundred rent-a-johnnies. *He is a giver!*

I cannot imagine spending two full weeks in our semi-watertight nylon hostel, let alone forty years. Wow, forty long years. Wandering in circles if the map in the front of my Bible is correct. Didn't somebody say, "Hey Moses, haven't we stayed at this KOA before?" "That mirage looks strangely familiar." "Are we there yet?" It is one thing to wander in the Super Wal-Mart for half of your life, but another thing to wander in the wilderness.

> The Guinness Book of World Records catalogs the world's longest tent camping experience as being over twenty-two years. People, if you're living in a tent for twenty-two years you're not camping; you're homeless.
> *Mike G. Williams*

If you study their story, you will find a murmuring people who had to learn a lot of lessons before they got to the resort property. I don't like that theology. It would be much nicer to take me first to the *Marriott*, and then we could sit down for some *casual* life lessons. But the truth is that I don't learn that way. I can be given information that way, but knowledge and understanding most often come from the wilderness experience itself. As much as I would hate to admit it, the things that I know that I know, I have learned from camping in the midst of the situation. The word today would be discipleship. It means a day in and day out, repetitive working-through of my faith, my growth, and my understanding. It's not easy this way. Nothing worth having ever comes easy.

> It is not true that "Nice Guys Finish Last." Studies have shown that, on the average, nice guys finish third in a field of six. Actually, short guys finish last. By the way, in medieval times, it was widely believed that nice guys finished twenty-sixth. You can see how limited those people were.
> *George Carlin*

I have no idea what wilderness you are in. I *can* challenge you to quickly learn the appointed lesson so you can get on with your life. So you can move onto the next *camping* experience. Be encouraged, for one day we will come forth from this wilderness experience called life and see the Grand Hotel on the horizon. The doorman will usher us into the ballroom for a great feast. We will sit next to the King. Hallelujah! And I hear that there will be free valet parking. Bonus!

**Prayer:** *Great Father, Leader of my life, guide me today. I open up my heart and mind to hear from You today. May I learn the lessons necessary for passage to the next phase of my life, and may I greet each step with anxious anticipation of what You will teach me. Amen.*

*The Lord has kept me alive these forty-plus years as we journeyed through the wilderness. Today I am eighty-five years old and I am still as strong as the day I started.*
Joshua 14:10

# 13

# They Say Florida Is Nothin' but Bugs

*Roaches must be the cleanest animals on earth, because every time I see them they are in the bathtub.*

Jimmy Walker

This Chicago boy spent his summer nights playing in the alleys and what few yards there were, capturing that amazing creature called the *lightning bug*. I now reside in Florida, where they are few and far between. But when I was a kid in Illinois, there were hundreds of them. We would take an old Hellmann's mayonnaise jar out into the yard and fill the thing with these miniature power plants. They would glow and glow. Later, as the oxygen in the jar would begin to run low, they would begin to die out. Mom would remind me to poke some holes in the top. So, with a few taps of a steak knife, they were glowing again. Fatigue would eventually set in, and their neon backpacks would wane. A good shaking would bring them back to bumpy life. Sometimes we would roll the jar down the dark alley like a big glowing wheel or play catch with a Haley's comet. *I know it was cruel, but these are bugs, people, so get over it!* An irritation of the jar always brought the bugs to their finest light.

> You christen a new ship by smashing a bottle of champagne over the front of it. You should not try this with a new pony...I thought the children would never stop crying.
>
> *Tim Jones*

It's interesting that Paul gives a similar analogy to the treasure of faith that believers hold in their heart. He calls it a great treasure that is housed in a fragile jar. A jar that cannot claim strength or longevity can only point to the beauty within. It is because of the enclosed treasure that our enemy would try to destroy us. Paul makes references to the fact that we are afflicted, but somehow not crushed. We are perplexed, but amazingly not driven to despair. We have been tossed around and scratched quite a bit, but we are still able to contain the great mystery of faith. All of this is possible because the light of God inside each one of us is greater than any outside force.

> Sometimes when I drive by the Optimist Club at night, I stop and let the air out of their car tires...I think it helps them weed out the hypocrites.
>
> *Mike G. Williams*

It is so amazing to think that the Creator of the universe would entrust his light to me. Oh yes, and to you as well. So do not be arrogant, oh ye of mayonnaise heritage. Don't be puffed up. Remember that your clothes are but a paper label that will deteriorate in a few washings. Be glad, rather, because you have been called and chosen to come out from under the sink and to be transparent. You have been chosen to be a vessel of honor for God.

**Prayer:** *Father, it is with great humility that I thank You for allowing me to be Your vessel. May the light I show come from Your truth. I graciously ask You to rub off my label so that I may illuminate more of You. Amen.*

*We have a treasure hidden in ordinary glass jars, this way it is made very clear that any extraordinary power belongs to God and does not come from us.*

2 Corinthians 4:7

**14**

# If the King James Version Was Good Enough for...

*Four out of five dentists are doing 80 percent of the dental work in this country and I don't think that is fair.*

Tim Jones

I grew up very poor. I know everybody says that. No, I did not walk seven miles to school in the snow with only one shoe that I would have to change halfway there to keep frostbite from taking over the naked foot. We did, however, only celebrate every other birthday. I was one year old, then I was three, and then I was five. *It really did save on expenses.* It was a little weird, though, when people would say, "How old are you?" My response was always something like, "I'm five, but I'm going to be seven." Which may be why they made me ride the short bus until I was in high school.

My son, who is four years old *and will soon be six*, loves the Christian video series *Bible Man*. Rarely does a day go by without my son sitting in front of the video player, quoting word for word everything Bible Man has to say. He has learned to quote more than thirty Bible verses from the *Caped Christian Crusader* over the past year. After each video episode, Chapman retreats to his room and returns with two swords I made for him out of PVC pipe. I covered them with foam because although he is only four, he can swing a sword like he's six. We have a standard sword fighting ritual. It is a reenactment of the famous

> Our favorite thing to do on Easter Sunday was to see what the rich kids were wearing, because we knew that's what we'd be wearing the next Easter.
>
> *Chonda Pierce*

Bible Man battle with the *Evil Fibbler*. It must be done meticulously. Chapman feeds me the lines and I repeat them, being careful not to miss a single word. I am called upon to deliver the climatic line before the battle's end. I look my son right in the mask and say, "You're nothing without the Bible!" To that, Chapman's eye glistens as he responds, "That's the nicest thing you've said to me all day." I then get walloped into oblivion. Out of the mouth of babes.

Where would I be without the word of God? What would I know of Jesus Christ? Where could I go for God's laws? I live in an era of spiritual illiteracy. I can count on one hand the close friends of mine who have read the Bible through even once in their life. I know it is tough! I grew up with the King James Version of 1611. No, no, not the one you have. The one before it was updated four times. The one that allows me to now interpret all the British dialogued PBS shows for my friends. *Yea beloved, 'tis those ones!* I can bequeath upon you a recitation of well over two hundred verses of Holy Writ from memory in old English! *That alone makes me quite a hit at parties.* It is a great tragedy that with all the new translations available to us in full color, we as a church are still biblically illiterate. I'm not mad or trying to be condemning. If I were mad I WOULD BE USING CAPITAL LETTERS! *I type way too much e-mail.* Rather, it breaks my heart that the jewel of the literary world goes unread. The all-time bestseller may be the least read.

> One man's pet-stained carpet is another man's twister game.
> *Mike G. Williams*

A good friend and great comedian, Justin Fennell, has a hilarious story called the *Southern Fried Preacher.* It is about a young preacher who, in his zeal to share all that he knows, inadvertently melts twenty-five Bible stories together. When you know the stories individually, you can quickly see the *montage* of biblical buffoonery. It would be similar to me saying, "Jack and Jill went up the hill, to fetch an itsy bitsy spider from Mother Hubbard's shoe in exchange for some curds and whey and some crazy glue for their pal Humpty Dumpty who had hurt himself playing with that little hyperactive firebug candle Jumping Jack." I asked Justin to perform *Southern Fried Preacher* one night as a guest at one of my concerts. While the crowd did not lack appreciation of Justin's gifted storytelling prowess, they just didn't know the Bible stories well enough to understand the humor. They loved Justin, but the story died. I felt so bad.

> Give a man a fish and you feed him for a day. Teach a man to use a net and he won't bother you for weeks.
> *Mike Atkinson*

What a privilege it is to have the Word of God so available to any of us. People of any language or educational background can find a translation for themselves. We have Bibles in Braille, Bibles on CD, Computer Bibles that download to your PDA. I personally like my son's Children's Bible. I'm not joking; it has little words and big pictures. *If you see any big words in my writing, you can bet an editor put them there.* The

Bible has been given to us as a gift from the Father. Cherish that gift. Make an effort to read one of the New Testament books every week. Sometimes I read Third John or Jude twice. I know what you are thinking, and the answer is yes, I'm just that spiritual!

**Prayer:** *Dear God in heaven, I thank You for the words of truth contained in the Bible. Help me to have the courage to read it daily, so that I may grow to be more like Jesus Christ. Reveal yourself, illuminate my paths, and correct my mistakes through Your blessed Word today. Amen.*

*All scripture is inspired by God and is profitable.*
2 Timothy 3:16

# 15

# Shut Up
# and Laugh

*Laughter is your best weapon. Keep the safety off, and don't take yourself too seriously.*

Dennis Miller

$\mathcal{J}$t was a good flight, and he struck up a conversation. "I'm a clinical psychologist. What do you do?" I hate to talk to these guys. I always feel like they are psychoanalyzing me, and that makes the real me feel very uncomfortable. *I want people to love me for whom I'm pretending to be.* We exchanged greetings and shared our work. I was giving him little humorous stories that he could use in his

> If you lend someone $20, and never see that person again, it was probably worth it.
>
> *Justin Fennell*

talks, and in exchange, he was giving me free help! *So, it was a win-win situation*. I asked him a question about an article I had just read in a medical journal, an article that claimed that laughing one hundred times a day was equivalent to a ten-mile jog for the heart muscle. Considering the fact that I can clearly see my enhanced abdominal region, I am prone to believe the health benefits are limited to the heart.

> Sometimes it's the little things that make a difference. A man walking down a busy city street, shouting and screaming to himself is not acceptable. Put a cell phone in his hand and he's just part of the crowd.
>
> *Taylor Mason*

He explained that laughter is a great medication, but since it cannot be bottled and sold, we will have to continue to medicate people. I immediately began trying to figure out a way to sell all my comedy CD's to an HMO. He shared a unique statistic with me that day. Four-year-olds average over one hundred laughs a day, while sixty-five-year-olds average only four laughs a day. Consider how that plays out in your life for just a minute. Our heart gets stronger as we laugh more, hmmm! But as we get older, we tend to laugh less. That really is a shame. Just think of the money I could save on Bayer aspirin in my senior years alone.

> He who laughs last probably didn't get it and is now merely succumbing to peer pressure and that makes me feel sad.
>
> *Mike G. Williams*

I was able to share with him the Bible verse about a merry heart being good like a medicine. He replied, "Oh, you are one of those Christians." "Yes," I responded, sensing the cynicism in his voice, "and here we are flying at thirty-two thousand feet above the surface of the earth, fighting the law of gravity with two engines built by underpaid, disgruntled factory workers and maintained by an angry mechanic one week away from a strike. Sir, I believe that if one of those engines decides to fail, you will become a Christian too." He smiled and said, "You are probably right!"

Let a merry heart be yours today. You will have to work at it. The enemy has come to steal your joy. Laugh at the guy who cuts you off on the way to work today. Laugh out loud. Laugh at the idiot with forty-six unpriced items in the express lane. Laugh at the driver in front of you who could have pulled out seven times but didn't because he was lighting a smoke, changing a cassette tape, and gawking at you in the mirror, all while having his head in his tailpipe, metaphorically speaking. Laugh! It's good exercise, and it's a God-thing. Practice it often. Laughter is Prozac for the soul!

**Prayer:** *God, assist me in finding humor in the mundane, simple, stupid, and aggravating things of life. May I find laughter on my journey and bring the medicine of laughter to others in a good and wholesome way. Amen.*

**A merry heart does a body good, like medicine.**
Proverbs 17:22

# 16

# Open Mouth, Insert Shoe

*I said she had a mind like a steel trap and she took it as a compliment; I meant that there were probably little furry animals in there desperately trying to chew their legs off.*

Tim Jones

**Y**ou don't sweat much for a fat guy," he said with an oblivious smile. "Thanks," I retorted, "You don't look scared for a guy who is about to get hit in the nose." Words can have a powerful effect on people. It was ten years ago that I took the stage for my first big event as a comedian. I was really nervous. It is one thing to entertain in front of your family and friends. It is another thing to step in front of six thousand unforgiving teenagers who have

> Never test the depth of the water with both feet.
> *Justin Fennell*

been promised that you were the funniest thing since the spontaneous combustion of a Barney doll. I had to take the stage with energy. God was with me—and three cappuccinos.

There I was, blasting through some really funny prop jokes, when the *situation* happened. As I pulled my third prop out of the box, my mind went totally blank. My third prop is one-half of a coat hanger, which I would usually interpret as being for people who like to shop at half-off sales. Well, instead of saying, "For people who like to shop at half-off sales," I said, "This is a coat hanger for a one-armed dude." It was a verbal snafu, but everyone roared with laughter; everyone except the fourteen-year-old boy with only one arm. He got up and left the room. It hit me hard when it happened. If I had a gun, I might have said, "And this is funny too," and shot myself. I was staggered to see how my words could have a negative effect on people. I'm supposed to be the funny man! The exhorter! When you leave my show, you are supposed to be feeling good about life and believing that God can do great things in you!

> If a picture is really worth a thousand words, what is the value of a picture of a thousand words? Or what about a picture of a picture containing a thousand words?
>
> *Mike G. Williams*

Now, I must say, there have been the wackos over the years! You know, the ones who are not playing with a full deck, yet still find a way to pay cab fares. These are the professionally offended. Maybe you have heard their protests: "You should not do jokes about chickens, because my brother was killed in a chicken accident"; "My uncle was mauled by a flamingo once, and I don't think flamingos are funny"; "I own a cat and I happen to like Chinese food." Every one of these statements have been made to me at some point in my career. *This is why I believe there should be mandatory medication services for some people.*

However, most of the criticism I have received over the years has been very gracious and well-taken. There have been a number of jokes that I have removed from my program. I did it because people have pointed out the offensiveness of them. *Each one of us has a different size of envelope to push.* I appreciate honest, constructive advice. I especially appreciate it when a person will share with a heart of love and kindness.

We all have the power of words at our disposal. The word of God reminds us in Matthew 12:36 to be careful of idle words. We must learn to bridle our tongues, for we will give an accounting. That is a very hard assignment for a guy who has the spiritual gift of humor and sarcasm. Okay, maybe they are not spiritual gifts, but they are gifts nonetheless. God has allowed me to make a living with them for the past twenty years. But bridle my tongue? Me? Impossible!

I watched a young man on one of the morning television shows who had vowed to remain silent for a year. He did use a computer keyboard to answer questions, though. He said, or rather typed, how much more people enjoyed being around him now that he could only listen. I hope people would not say that about me. I pray that my words are words that edify the community. I pray that I season the humor with kind words of encouragement. I hope that I have used my two ears more than my one mouth.

> I recently had a ringing in my left ear. The doctors looked inside and found a small bell.
>
> *George Carlin*

Will you join me today in a challenge? When you have a chance to say an offensive or hurtful word, bite down extremely hard on your tongue. The pain will erase the words that you were going to say. They will probably be replaced by some new words, so you may have to bite down again. It's a workable solution when you consider that an actual bridle is so cumbersome and un-aesthetically pleasing. They don't make tongue bridles like they used to.

I was able to spend some quality time that weekend with the one-armed boy and allow my tongue to be used to encourage and build up. That young man taught me some good lessons. *These tongues can be so versatile. If you don't have one, order one today.*

**Prayer:** *Dear God, may the words that flow from my mouth be acceptable to You. I desire to be a communicator of joy and a distributor of comfort. Help me today. Amen*

*May the words of my mouth and the meditations of my heart be acceptable in Your sight.*
Psalms 19:14

**17**

# I Used to
# Remember Things—
# I Think

*There are three things you need to be successful in life.*
*Unfortunately, I don't know what they are.*

Taylor Mason

*I* used to drink a lot of Diet Coke, and a friend of mine told me that Diet Coke contains aspartame. Laboratory studies show that aspartame causes short-term memory loss. Now, short-term memory loss is not something that I really need. Can you see me getting up in front of a crowd and just standing there saying, "Uhhhh???" So, I do not drink Diet Coke anymore.

> They say your memory is the first thing to go, and I can't quite remember what the other things were.
>
> *Justin Fennell*

> Sometimes I experience Alzheimer's and *deja vu* at the same time and get that eerie feeling that I'm forgetting something all over again.
>
> *Tim Jones*

To be real honest with you, I have the memory retention of a fallen pine cone. I always have good intentions of remembering stuff. But, well, you know. Hey, the fact that I can remember having good intentions shows a marked improvement.

I have very selective memory. I can remember the latest college basketball scores. I can remember my son's birthday. I can remember the chords to three or four hundred songs. I can remember to take my keys out of the ignition when I leave the car almost every time now. I remember to put clothes on before leaving the house. I remember to slow down when I see a squad car. I remember to eat meals. *I'm very good at that one.* I'm sure I'm forgetting something here. Well, I could go on, but I will not. I try to blame my poor memory on the fact that I used to drink Diet Coke. A friend of mine told me that some chemical in the Diet Coke would cause memory loss. I can't seem to remember which chemical it was at this moment.

I believe God must drink Diet Coke. He has all the *classic* signs. My memory is bad, but God doesn't remember half the stuff I tell Him. When we confess our sins to Him, He forgives us and disposes of those sins into the depths of the sea. He says they will never be remembered against us again. On the other hand, certain members of *my* circle of influence, I'm not saying whom, *my spouse*, have been known to remind me of past goof-ups. God

> A recent survey said that the majority of the population did not want to live past the age of 90. Obviously none of the people surveyed were 89 at the time.
>
> *Mike G. Williams*

promises to forgive the past and forget it totally. We may remind Him of our failures, but He just scratches His head. Once, I tried to convince my spouse that I am not really forgetful, I'm just like the Lord.

I do believe it is *good for me* to remember my past. It helps me not to repeat the same mistake twice. Those who cannot remember the past are forced to repeat it! My eighth grade history teacher taught me that line the hard way. *I was the oldest boy in the class the following year.* Each day I ask God to forgive me of the sins that I remember and the many I forget. Each day He does and allows me to stand before Him with clean hands and a pure heart. I'm glad I don't forget to ask for forgiveness. That would

> The wisest man I ever knew taught me some things I never forgot. And although I never forgot them, I never quite memorized them either. So what I'm left with is the memory of having learned some very wise things that I can't quite remember.
>
> *George Carlin*

be a bummer. My memory is not all that good. You see, I used to drink a lot of Diet Coke and somebody was saying something about that. Oh yes, it caused some kind of memory problems, I think. Well, I'm sure it will come to me later.

It is marvelous to know that my confessed past will never dawn on God later. When we confess our sins, God forgives and forgets. What a promise. What a Savior! One day, I will stand before Him, and Jesus will present me to the Father and to the family as Mike G. Williams, the perfect one. I will just look at my wife and smile! *The G stands for good.*

**Prayer:** *Our Father in heaven, I confess my sins to You. The ones I plainly remember and the ones I did not even realize I committed. You have seen every action and viewed every thought. There is so much forgiveness needed. Forgive me now. And thanks for forgetting those things You can't recall. Amen.*

*I will remember their sins no more.*
Hebrews 8:12

*He shall present you faultless before the presence of His glory with exceeding joy.*
Jude 1:24

# 18

# Read My Lips...
# No New Taxes!

*By your actions, I can conclude that you believe W.W.J.D. means, What Would Judas Do!*

Mike G. Williams

romise Keepers is an excellent organization, and I have had the thrill of speaking at many of their events. These are men who are standing up to a challenge and keeping their promises. But I got to thinking. What about the millions of men who are not spiritually ready to be Promise Keepers? They've never kept even the simplest of promises. These men may be on the way, but not quite there yet. For them, I will be starting a national campaign called *Premise Keepers*. Yes, Premise with an "e." It will be for men who need encouragement in keeping even a part of a promise. Men who promised they would be home for dinner and did not do it. Yet, they were home for dinner the next day. They kept the premise of the promise. And what about those men who can't commit? Those men who through years of baggage and undisciplined living do not even bother to make promises? For them, I will start *Promise Makers*. It will be dedicated to helping men phrase and articulate an actual promise. They will not be responsible for the keeping of it, but just the making of it. I understand that to many of you, this may not seem like much, but it is a start.

> Don't ever miss a good chance to simply shut up.
> *Justin Fennell*

My dad used to talk about letting your yea be yea and your nay be nay. I thought he was talking pig Latin. I understand now that he was talking about being honest and keeping your promises. I have come to know he swiped the quote from book of James. It is so easy to lie. Even those misleading truths that flow from an author's pen—or keyboard in my case. Consider the paragraph above. When I said I had the privilege of speaking at a Promise Keepers event, you were thinking about thousands of people. I was thinking about the local PK breakfast that was attended by well over twenty people. Would that be a yea-yea or a nay-nay? Probably neither.

Are you a person of your word? Think about it for a minute. Are you a person of your word? "Relatively honest," you say? That is a fair answer from the dude in the plaid sport coat, green tie, and blatant denial. How would you rate in

> There are two theories about arguing with a woman. Neither one works.
> *Will Rogers*

accordance to the truth, the whole truth, and nothing but the truth, so help me, please? I would be pleading the Fifth Amendment. Any answer I give could be used against me, blah, blah, and blah.

My wife has taken and given all of those personality type tests. I turned out to be an ID. I have no ID-ea what that means exactly. *Sorry.* I am told that it makes *fun* and *getting along* a major player in my personality. She, on the other hand, is a truth-teller. She has the ability to get in someone's face and be honest. I do not. I would tell Burt Reynolds and Ernest Angley that I thought their hairpieces looked extremely natural. *Then I would secretly send them a few coupons for a free carpet cleaning and hope they got the message.*

A major tenant of the Christian faith is truth. Jesus claimed to be truth personified, and if we are going to be like Him, we must be as well. Let's try it for a day. You may have to use creative honesty when your boss asks you about his new tie. Say, "I clearly believe your new tie is made with the finest quality material available and certainly represents the person you really are...Rock on, boss!" Go the whole day with your nose clean and our mouth honest. I believe we can do it together.

**Prayer:** *Lord, may I be honest for the next twenty-four hours. Amen.*

*Do not lie. Let your "Yes" be yes and your "No" be no, so that you do not fall under condemnation.*
James 5:12

# We Love to Fly
# and It Shows

*Abe Lincoln had a brighter future when he picked up his
tickets at the box office.*

Kelsey Grammer

*H*ere I sit in the stinkin' airport again. I arrived at
8:30 A.M., and I'm still here at 2:00 P.M. Those
who fly Delta Airlines call the Atlanta Hartsfield Airport
"Purgatory." On a bad weather day, this place can get really
cranky really quick. Tempers are short, and people are ready to
get in your face for no apparent reason. I'm sure the service
center workers would like to have some aerosol Valium at
their disposal. I can just hear them saying, "Next in line
please, and breathe deeply." I have just walked for half a block
to find a power plug so I can do a little more work on the book

you're reading. I could go to the Crown Room, but I am stuck out on Concourse D where the amenities are limited to a small *Burger King* with poor kitchen ventilation. It smells like your plane is on fire when they fire up the broiler.

I'm hoping to get to Rochester, New York before my concert is over. I believe I have a fifty-fifty chance at this point. We have a plane. We have flight attendants. We are waiting on a pilot. There are two here in the waiting area, but they only have two stripes each, and I have been told you need three stripes to fly this plane. I suggested that we let the one sit on the other's lap, and that would give us a total of four stripes. This would give us an overqualified pilot, but I'm okay with that. My idea got a good laugh, but was rejected by the red coat. On a bright note, Delta has given each one of us a Sky-deli snack. It is a small cheese and cracker combination, a warm yogurt and a bag of chips. They keep it fresh by delivering it in a plastic-lined airsickness bag. The bag will come in handy for anyone venturing past the yogurt cap. The gate agents deceptively give us hopeful announcements every couple of minutes.

> When someone is impatient and says, "I haven't got all day," I always wonder how can that be? How can you not have all day?
>
> *George Carlin*

It is very interesting to sit here and watch people. I enjoy people-watching, or in this case, hostage-watching. Over near the counter are the angry and bitter people blurting out their discouragement and disbelief at every announcement. I believe from their current facial shade that their blood pressure medicine is already in the cargo hold. We have the sleepers, who have curled up by themselves in the corner, seemingly oblivious to our plight. There's a mom trying to keep her young child entertained for four hours with a sock puppet. A few passengers have opened up to total strangers, sharing their lives and pictures of the grandkids. A few read books. Some are across the aisle in the smoking lounge calming their nerves, while others are down the hall at the bar. I guess they need a greater degree of calming. I sit here munching on my Sky-deli, minus the yogurt, of course, and typing a few salient thoughts.

I can't help but notice that every time the door to the jetway opens, everyone looks up with anticipation. It doesn't even have to open completely. A simple jiggle of the handle can excite the crowd and get me to click the *save to disk* icon. We are all waiting impatiently for the intercom to declare that a pilot has arrived and it's time to board. I'm ready.

What a microcosm of the Christian life, *in a far-reaching, rabbit-chasing way*. Here we are crammed into this waiting room called life. Waiting for our Captain to arrive and fire up the plane for home. It's been a long adventuresome wait, and we have grown impatient from time to time. Yet, we cling to an unnatural hope. Our spirit is revitalized by every coded update hidden in the evening news. It's as if we can hear the distant thunder. I can hardly wait to hear Gabriel saying, "We will begin our boarding of flight 777 with first class, and then from the rear of the shuttle forward. Please have your tickets in hand." *I will be waving my ticket, baby. We are going home.*

Days like these make me join in with old John and say, "even so Lord Jesus, come quickly." But bad days can be improper motives. I never want to get Christ's coming confused with escapism. There is so

> DELTA is an acrostic for Doesn't Ever Leave The Airport.
> *David Edwards*

much work to be done while we wait. There are missions to complete, and we must not grow complacent. The return of Christ is more than saying goodbye to the problems of this world. It is the glorious union that has awaited us for so long. The day we see our Savior. Hallelujah, Oh what a Savior He is! But until that day, you will hear me humming, "Somewhere over the rainbow, skies are blue, birds fly over the rainbow, tell me why can't I?" I'm ready and I know you are too, Mom. Hang in there.

**Prayer:** *Dear Father, I anxiously await the day in which You turn to Gabriel and give him the high sign. The day that You send our Captain Jesus Christ to take us home. May we live this day in the light of His imminent return, Amen.*

*For the Lord himself shall descend from heaven with a shout, the dead in Christ shall rise and we which are alive and remain shall be caught up to be with the Lord forever.*
1 Thessalonians 4:17

**20**

# Goldilocks Was
# a Dirty Thief

*Becoming aware of my character defects leads me to the next step. That is of blaming my parents.*

Mike Atkinson

$\mathcal{I}$ always loved that story of the little girl, the bears, and the porridge. When I was a little boy, I remember being scared that the bears were going to come home and maul Goldilocks at any moment. When I was a teenager, I thought that would be funny. I might have even paid to see it happen! But as I look back on the story, I see the entire story in a different light. I view an entirely different moral dilemma.

> What's mine is mine and what's yours is negotiable.
>
> *Dave Roever*

Out of the box, you have this rogue girl out in the woods who breakes into the unsuspecting home of a kindly bear family. She goes right to their kitchen and begins to eat their porridge. I'm not a bear, but I imagine that porridge is pretty hard to come by. Here you are living on twigs and berries and an occasional slow-moving camper, and then surprise—somebody leaves a can of porridge at the neighboring KOA, along with a can opener. What a find! You have saved it for a special occasion, maybe a birthday or anniversary, and now a young, spoiled, gets-everything-she-wants rich girl comes gallivanting through your hideout. If that's not bad enough, she goes on to break your little cub's wooden rocker. The one you ordered from Cracker Barrel. Does she fix it? Leave a note? Offer to replace the chair? No, she heads upstairs to see what kind of damage she can do to the bedroom. Tired from her hooligan lifestyle, she decides to take a nap. Are you still rooting for the safety of our little darling?

> I like to sit behind people with hearing aids and blow a tiny high pitched dog whistle. I've always liked to do that.
> *Mike G. Williams*

Why did I find myself hoping the blatant, unremorseful lawbreaker escapes before Papa Bear comes home? I find myself doing that in movies as well. The bad guy becomes the good guy. "Run, the cops are right behind you!" I squall. When did I get things so turned around? When did I go from "run, Forest, run" to "run, Hannibal, run"? For the record, I have never cheered for the shirtless, drunk guys on *Top Cops*. I just wanted you to know that. I would like the coyote to get that roadrunner just once though before they leave syndication!

> I broke my ankle mountain climbing on a relief map. I fell off the kitchen table.
> *Steven Wright*

In a day when eternal black and white have been merged to an eerie gray, it behooves us to remember our calling. We have been called to walk the straight path, cheering on the righteous and encouraging the faithful. Our life is to be a stirring testament to God's sustaining grace. Whoops, I started writing a Steve Green song, and if I went any further it would be plagiarism. *Please don't encourage me.* We must refuse to let our guard down. We must return to cheering for the good guys. We must support the ones who stand up to the tyranny of liberal morals and feel-good philosophy. We must curse the movies that move us to applaud infidelity and incest. We must return to the virtues of *It's a Wonderful Life* and renounce so-called *American Beauty*. It is American degeneracy.

Where have you allowed your guard to be let down? Maybe it's in your thought life. Maybe it's in your prayer life. Maybe it was in the simple neglect of cheering for the good guys. I want to encourage you to see wrong for what it is. To see evil in any form the way God sees it—heartbreaking.

**Prayer:** *Forgive me Father, for letting this world's value system corrupt my thinking. I have forgotten that You are for the good guy. Let me weep once again for those good and moral things that have fallen by the wayside. Let me weep for the things that make You weep. Amen.*

*Happy is the man who does not follow the advice of the wicked or take the road that they tread. A happy man's delight is in the law of the Lord and he ponders those laws day and night.*
Psalms 1:1-2

# Lassie, Go Home

*My mother said, "You won't amount to anything because you procrastinate." I said, "You just wait."*

Judy Tenuta

*a*m I crazy, or is stupidity running rampant in this country? *I heard your mumbled answer, and that wasn't nice.* Television takes the Golden Globe in this category. It seems that television ratings go from S for *stupid* to M for *mature* with nothing in the middle. If you were unaware, *mature* is a Hollywood term that means *filthy*. Some production houses have successfully combined mature and stupid into one under-cooked Hudson beef patty. Originally, I thought this dumbward spiral started with my generation. Afraid not! *For your information, dumbward is my variation on the word downward.*

So there I sat, watching TV Land in the hotel breakfast nook. There was the American classic, Lassie. Do you remember this show? It had three basic characters: Lassie, the world's smartest dog, Timmy, the world's dumbest boy child, and Timmy's Mom. She was the only woman in the world who could speak fluent Collie. Every week it was the same scenario. Timmy would find himself ten miles from the house, duct taped to a bag of concrete in the trunk of Jimmy Hoffa's limo. *A freak duct tape accident, I don't have all the details.* Lassie would watch him do this. After a brief struggle, Lassie would run home to get help. Around the curve of the road and up onto the porch, the pooch would come. The dog would then open the screen door with her paw. Apparently, Lassie had *opposable thumbs*. Bounding into the kitchen, Lassie would bark, "Woof, woof, woof, woof, rrrroof." Mom would look up from her own cooking and declare, "Oh my, Timmy has duct taped himself to a bag of concrete in the trunk of Jimmy Hoffa's limo! Let me quickly turn off the stove, check the iron, and change into something more comfortable. Then we will all get into the truck and let Lassie drive us to the fresh concrete pour behind the Giants stadium."

When the general public finally caught on to this blatant display of asininities, they gave us a new sitcom called *Flipper*! Flipper was a swimming Lassie. They put Lassie in a wet suit and said, "You know the plot, do it, Girl." A few years later,

> Drug dogs smell so much cocaine each day, that they become addicted to the stuff. I can see it now: "I don't want any ALPO, let's go to work, c'mon cop'er man, let's get to work early today, ruff-ruff." Then you have to send your dog to the Betty Ford kennel!"
> *Mike G. Williams*

> Can't we find our inner child...and give him a good spanking?
> *Dennis Miller*

we were presented with *Gentle Ben*. Duh, gentle and grizzly bear are two incongruent words. This was not a gentle bear. This was a highly medicated bear! Gentle Ben became the poster bear for the Yellowstone chapter of N.A.

Could it be time for us to come back to some basic intelligence in this country? Whoops, I think I spelled intelligence wrong. *Spell Check*. Okay, I fixed it. Maybe intelligence is the wrong word. I guess I am looking for the word "wisdom." God-given wisdom will produce intelligence and morals. Hollywood occasionally throws us what they consider to be a religious bone with *Touched By An Angel* or *Seventh Heaven*. Thanks! Sometimes I feel like the whole country has loaded up in the *short bus* for a moonlight cliffside ride with the crash test dummies at the wheel.

> Don't ever get CPR and VCR mixed up. Because when someone is having a heart attack, the last thing they need is you trying to shove a tape in their mouth.
>
> *Tim Jones*

Has there ever been a time that we needed wisdom any more than today? Our streets are strewn with the waste of uneducated decisions and moronic mistakes. Our prisons are full of the repercussions of lousy choices. Christians are often at the forefront of the parade. I have been a Grand Marshall! I could not find a notebook large enough to record the mistakes of my past. The times I lacked wisdom and I did not even bother to ask for wisdom are too many to list. If I would only call on God for wisdom at every turn, what a difference it could make.

The good news is that wisdom is readily available. Yes, we will have to put away our pride and ask for help. This is hard for a man who won't even ask for directions to the highway. But we need to get over it. We love to give directions, so why can't we affirm someone and ask for directions? There are godly counselors and pastors a phone call away. We have the Bible, if we care to dig for ourselves. We have the Spirit to guide us if we ask. Best of all is the promise that we can have some wisdom if we simply ask for it. That is almost too simple. Why didn't I think of that?

**Prayer:** *Dear Father, I need wisdom and understanding to make good decisions this day. The questions before me are complicated and many. I need Your divine guidance and strength to follow through in what You lead me to do. Amen.*

*If any man lacks wisdom let him ask of God who gives wisdom graciously to all who ask.*
James 1:5

# Mirror, Mirror
# On the Wall

*Body-piercing. A powerful, compelling visual statement that says, "Gee...in today's competitive job market, what can I do to make myself even more unemployable?"*

Dennis Miller

*D*o you remember the era when guys carried those purse-looking things they called shoulder bags? They were the forerunners of the modern backpack movement. I have a leather briefcase. I have no briefs, just the case. It makes me feel powerful and important. Clothing styles change way too often. *I believe women's styles change every time my wife goes to the mall.* I used to own a pair of bell-bottoms so big you could house missionaries on furlough in them. They were especially well suited for shoplifting spaghetti from the grocery store. Of course, everyone knows that you need a stovepipe hat to swipe the sauce. I was a *poor Bible college* student back then. *Not really, I just wanted to say that to get a rise out of you.* I still have an old tie-dye shirt that a friend of mine brought me from Jamaica. I don't wear it anymore, especially since Jerry passed. *Could we get a moment of silence?*

> I just can't believe those tribal people they show on National Geographic really stand in front of a mirror and say, "Dude, this eight-inch chunk of cedar tree imbedded in my lower lip and this pig bone in my ear look really attractive. I will be a chick magnet at the rain dance tonight."
>
> *Mike G. Williams*

Sometimes I will watch the History channel. I enjoy our 20/20 hindsight. I also enjoy the VH-1 program called *Where Are They Now*. It encourages me to know that the superstars of my teen years are now sitting at home in their worn-out underwear, wondering what to do with the rest of their lives. They are just like me! *Okay, I am not wondering what to do with the rest of my life.* I do enjoy looking back at the old styles of cars, clothes, and haircuts. *Vintage* and *retro* are the cliché words of the day. Have you ever really looked at your old grade school pictures? At what point did we walk out of the barbershop and say, "Hey, I look good like this"? Had I been drugged? Hypnotized? I looked like a stinking beaver. And plaid pants on a fat guy! What was up with that? I guess the hanging of mirrors in dressing rooms was not extremely popular back then.

> How much make-up should a real Christian woman wear? Well it really depends on her face.
>
> *Mike Warnke*

James tells us a story about a guy who looks in the mirror and walks away and forgets what he looked like. *That must have been my problem.* James compares it to a person who hears the word of God and does not respond to it. He says they deceive their own selves. They hear the truth. They view it face-to-face. Yet they walk away and forget what they saw. It sounds to me an awful lot like Sunday morning. My pastor delivers a wonderfully instructional message from God and I shout, "AMEN!" Well, I don't shout "amen," but I do occasionally mumble "amen" when prompted by my wife. I can truly agree with the *truth* in the message but continue to live in the *false*. I refuse to be changed by it, no matter how really ugly my present state is.

It is a scary thing to see myself in the mirror of God's word. To see myself naked and exposed for whom I really am. It's only then that I can know the full potential of what I can be through God's extreme grace—something different. The mirror is not there to propagate condemnation; rather, it is there to communicate the possibilities of my marked improvement. So look deep into the Word and see your possibilities, and don't forget them. My dad used to say, "Quit fooling yourself." I always wondered how a person could do that and now I know.

**Prayer:** *Holy Father, allow me to see myself as You see me. Allow me to see past all the lies that I have been telling others and those lies that I have come to believe myself. I am going to need Your help, maybe even a miracle to be changed. Do not let me forget and live in apathy to Your perfect plan in my life. And thank You for the death of paisley. Amen.*

*A person who hears the Word and does not obey the Word, is like a man who looks into the mirror and walks away and immediately forgets how ugly he looked.*
James 1:23-24

## 23

# Huked on Fonix
# Wurk'd Four Me

*Always take a good look at what you're about to eat. It's not really important to know what it is, but it's imperative to know what it was.*

Justin Fennell

*I* had made Webster's newest edition! I unashamedly take credit for starting the word *religiosity*. I blurted it out in the middle of a sermon for the first time in 1980. Later my friends asked, "What in the world is religiosity?" I came up with a quick definition that didn't meet their approval. I continued to use the word, making it a part of my vocabulary. Years later, my wife and I sat glued to the television set, watching a Billy Graham crusade. The Rev. Graham proclaimed, "Through their own religiosity." I leaped off the couch! I was vindicated! And by none other than the greatest evangelist this nation has ever known. All the years of postulating this word as an alternative to *religious legalism* had paid off. I had made history! *Let me bask in my own little fantasy for a moment please.*

My fascination with words started in school. I loved letters. I have to confess that for three years I was *hooked on phonics*. It started out with the easy vowels, and they became the gateway to the hard consonants. Before I could get help, I found myself slipping into the boys' room between classes to scratch a few letters on the aluminum walls. I would stay up all night listening to the *ABC song* backwards and watching *Conjunction Junction* videos. I was an addict. I finally got help, though. I am in a twelve-step group for *alphabetaholics*. It's not called AA or anything like that, because that's what we're trying to get away from.

> If at first you don't succeed, try, try, again. Unless of course you lost a limb on the first try! Then it's just best to admit your shortcomings.
> *Dave Hopping*

Letters make words, words create phrases, phrases convey thoughts, and thoughts move people. Wow, I can't believe I wrote that sentence and the spelling and grammar check accepted it! *My mouth is powerful. I am mouth: hear me roar!* When I was a kid, my mom used to add a line to the *Be Careful Song*. She would sing, "Be careful little larynx what you say…" It was too phonetically challenging to include the words *vocal chords*. But we got the message.

> You'll never hear this in Las Vegas: "Well, there goes the last of the Nobel Prize Money, papa…"
> *Taylor Mason*

Jesus taught us that the mouth is the gateway to the stomach, but the heart is gateway to the mouth (voice). I can know what you put in your mouth by putting a stethoscope to your stomach. And I can know what is in your heart by putting a microphone to your mouth. I'm afraid that I must have a very sarcastic heart. What about yours? What is coming from your mouth and thus, your heart? How would your co-workers answer that question?

I would like to think I have a healthy heart. I jog and take vitamins for my heart every day. I vicariously participate with the people on television doing their exercises with *Jake*. I empathize with Richard Simmons. I always watch *Walker Texas Ranger* do the *Bow Flex* commercials and promise to buy one someday. I drink at least eight glasses of water a week. I eat healthily, and as the late Rev. Charles H. Spurgeon said, "I try to keep my cigars to a maximum of four per day." Maybe that's why he's now, late. *Pardon the humorous quote*! If my heart were examined solely on the words of my mouth, would you find it healthy?

Straight to the point! Fill your heart with the living word of God, flood it with worship and praise, massage it with the oil of the spirit and gladness, exercise it with service, and the mouth will bear witness. If you feed your heart with garbage, your mouth will deliver garbage back. A wise man once told me to *drive a library*. He explained how we spend hundreds of hours in our cars listening to mindless chatter, when we could be using that radio and tape player to make ourselves *Masters of the Word*. No, I think he phrased it, "Let the Word master us." Either way would be a bonus! Think about what you are filling yourself with today?

> The old saying goes, if you can't say something good, don't say anything at all. Which makes me believe that mimes must be an angry and bitter lot.
> *Mike G. Williams*

**Prayer:** *Dear Holy Father, I love You. Help me guard my heart so that my mouth may speak good things. Protect me from the negative influences around me that seek to destroy me and those I love. May the words I deliver this day come from the areas of my heart that are given to You. Please continue to work on me. Amen.*

*It's not what goes into your mouth that defiles a person, but it is what comes out of the mouth that defiles.*
Matthew 15:11

# 24

# Okay, So I Need
# A Little Therapy

*I tried Flintstone vitamins. I didn't feel any better, but I
could stop the car with my feet.*

Joan St. Once

*I*t was a few years ago when I realized how sick I really
am. I'm talking about my mind. You see, I just
thought I was a normal, white American male until I spent an
afternoon with a Shrink. Don't worry, I did not pay for this. I
may be a nut, but I am a thrifty nut. We were huddled in an
airport waiting area, and I had nothing better to do than try a
few new jokes on the lady sitting next to me. She let me know
that through my humor she could tell that I had a very trou-
bled past. She asked me to tell her my story. Of course I did;
she claimed to have a Ph.D.

Well, it turns out that I am a fully-operating, dysfunctional, co-dependent, homosapien with protestant tendencies. Who knew? I wish my mom had told me. Maybe a schoolteacher or one of my currently unemployed high school guidance counselors should have said something. I should have known about this. It explains so many things. It gives me a whole new set of questions. I'm glad she explained to me that homosapien means human. At least I'm not an alien. *Well, at least that's what I led her to believe.*

It makes me feel better knowing that there is a reason for my madness. It's not my fault. None of this is my fault. It was in my gene pool and my adolescent fertilizer. This can't be biblical. I mean, how could God allow me to come from this soil? I mean, how could God allow such greatness to come from such fragile and humble beginnings? Shouldn't I be feeling some nausea or dizziness? I think I need to lie down.

Upon closer inspection of the Bible, I believe that I am in good company. Look at a few of the Old Testament boys for a minute. Abraham had two sons to two different women, and they all lived in the same tent. Either they were a little whacked out, or old Abe was the first Mormon. His young son, Isaac, had to be ready for a few ink blot sessions after Abraham invited him to attend that combination campout/sacrifice trip. "Where's the sacrifice, Dad, and why are you carrying that duct tape and gasoline?" Isaac had a boy named Jacob the deceiver, who went on to have twelve sons. *Some people should not procreate in the first place, much less twelve times.* Ten of these brothers ganged up to throw number eleven,

> In Italy's thirty years under the Borgias, they had warfare, terror, and murder, but they produced Michelangelo, Leonardo da Vinci, and the Renaissance.
> In Switzerland, they had brotherly love, five hundred years of democracy and peace, and what did they produce?
> The Cuckoo Clock.
> *Orson Welles*

> I wish people would learn to like me for who I'm pretending to be.
> *Mike G. Williams*

Joseph, into a well, and eventually sold him into slavery. *Hmmm, are we ready for a group session yet?*

On the other hand, Abraham became Father of Faith, and Isaac was the Son of Promise. Jacob became Israel, Prince with God. Joseph rose beyond his tragic circumstances and went on to save a nation. He ended up saving the very brothers who did these terrible things to him. He was so co-dependent and definitely a full-fledged enabler.

Toward the end of Joseph's story in the Bible, he makes this miraculous statement: "What man meant for evil God meant for good. God used the evil in my past to place me where I could preserve life." Wow, that makes me think that there may be a purpose for my past. It may simply be so that I can have compassion on others in my situation, or it may be that God has much more complicated plans for me. I wonder what God may have in store for you. What has He allowed you to be prepared for? *Okay, I mean right after a little therapy.*

**Prayer:** *Father in heaven, I call upon You now. You know my story and all the reasons for it, right or wrong. I ask that You turn my past into passion and my sicknesses into compassion. Heal my wounds that I may be able to heal others in Your name. Amen.*

*God used the evil in my past to bring me to a place where I could preserve life.*
Genesis 45:5

# 25

# He's Got A Gun

*The journey of a thousand miles begins with just one broken fan belt and a leaky radiator.*

Justin Fennell

M y dad was not the most patient man I ever knew, a WWII vet and proud of it. You know the type. I never saw him put on an old shirt to work on a car either. He loved cars, so to put on an old shirt was almost an insult to union craftsmanship. He dug right into that big V-8, in whatever he was wearing, at the first sign of a shaky idle. Now, he would always take his shirt off once he got it greasy, but I never remember him taking a shirt off first to avoid ruining it. Mom would yell out the window lovingly, "Honey why don't you take your shirt off before you ruin another one?" It was useless.

That was Dad. We often stopped so Dad could get a new shirt on the way to a wedding or funeral because he stopped at the last light to fine tune the carburetor. Maybe that's why I hate automotive work to this day. I won't even check the oil.

My dad was also a helpful man. He has spent months in the hospital from putting his back out working on somebody's car. I can remember the Christmas Eve day that my dad stopped to help a family. They were driving to Iowa to spend the holidays with their family. It could have been a simple flat tire, but it was a water pump. Dad dug into the engine while Mom went to a junkyard to get them a replacement. A few greasy hours later, we departed that corner parking lot. There was no charge and no gifts were accepted. We were four hours late to our family gathering, but everyone understood. They all knew my parents. Fortunately, my dad received a new shirt as a Christmas present that year.

> Everyone's always looking out for number one, unless they are walking through a cow pasture, then everyone is looking out for number two.
>
> *Tim Jones*

So, I guess helping out came quite naturally to me that January morning on I-75. My wife and I were motoring down the highway to a missions conference in Cincinnati, Ohio. We drove a big brown *Revcon* motor home at the time. Twenty-six feet of dark wood paneling and corduroy stretched over a 1971 *Oldsmobile Toranado* frame. *Yes, it was front-wheel drive.* I was in the driver's seat navigating the big boy in and out of the traffic when my wife yelled, "Look there's a guy beating up a lady in that car on the side of the road!" I swerved across two lanes of traffic and began the arduous task of backing up on the shoulder. When I got about sixty feet from them, I jumped out of the big pig and ran back to the car. It turned out to be two men in a jumble of fists and arms. So I grabbed a door handle, pulled it open, and yelled, "Everybody out of the car!" *I am nothing if not contemplative, introspective, and relatively stupid.* "He's got a gun,"

I hear coming from the churning bodies. One of the men bolted from the car and started running toward the motor home. Running toward the motor home that I had left running with the door open. Duh! "He's got a gun," the man in the car exclaimed! Here I am, a fat boy in a big goose down jacket, trying to run into the forty-mile-per-hour wind to chase a thin guy with no jacket who is supposed to have a gun. My wife is trying desperately to get the door closed before he gets there, but the wind is working the door like a giant sailboat. Can you feel the tension? *You could actually hear the Jaws theme playing in the background at the time.*

Well, she got the door closed and locked just before he grabbed the handle and pulled hard. Then he ran off into the field. It was a close call. It seems that this driver gave a lift to an escaped convict. The convict wanted total possession of the car about the time that we came along. We helped the poor motorist into our four-wheeled mobile home and cleaned his face and made him some coffee. We got to share the love of Christ that day by our words and our deeds. So it was a good day.

I don't think I need to explain any more, but I do hope you will take time to read the whole story of the Good Samaritan found in Luke chapter 10. It can be unnerving to

Delta Airlines ends each flight with the public service announcement, "As you continue your travel we encourage you to wear seatbelts whenever possible." As if we would not have thought of this on our own! We have seen those little straps in our car, and now, thanks to Delta's pre-flight demonstration and post-flight announcement, we are going to take a leap of safety faith and try them out. Maybe get them installed on the couch, my bicycle, the toilet seat. The possibilities are endless. Thanks Delta!

*Mike G. Williams*

help nowadays. Who wants to stop for the car on the side of the road anymore? We have Police, Safety Patrols, cell phones, and AAA to take care of things like that. But do we realize how many people are being held hostage right in our own backyard? We have our lawn-care man who has to drink himself to sleep each night, and next door is a working mother addicted to those little white pills. What about that traveling salesman who survives another week in his hotel room on a diet of porn and cigarettes? Your golf buddy's marriage is on the rocks and your jogging friend has cancer? And in this corner, weighing in at ninety-four pounds, is you. What can you do? *Good Samaritans die every day. I have my family to think about!* Yes, you do have a family to set an example for. What kind of example have you set?

Yes, there is a humorous moral to my story, and it goes like this. If you are ever driving a front-wheel drive motor home in the southbound lane of I-75 on a windy January day heading to a mission conference in Cincinnati, keep your eyes on the road; you don't want to miss a good fight. And in this gated community of my life, I need to reach out to those who are in need and invest in their lives. I need to be more like my earthly dad, and my heavenly Father.

**Prayer:** *God, protect me as I reach out to others in the way that I would want them to reach out to me. I desire to be careful yet caring. Protect me and give me ways to physically demonstrate Your love and mercy to the world. Amen.*

*You shall love your neighbor as yourself.*
Mark 12:31

# 26

# Hulk-O-Mania

*I have as much authority as the Pope, I just don't have as
many people who believe it.*

George Carlin

*a* few days ago, I was in a line at the airport and this
guy ran in from outside and cut to the front of the
line. He yelled to the gate agent about needing to get on a
flight that was already taxiing down to the runway. She very
kindly explained that she couldn't do that. He was furious, and
used a number of uniquely caustic adjectives in some rather
original sequences to let everyone know. He then flashed his
*Million Mile Flyer* card in her face and yelled, "You stupid lady,
do you know what this means?" The flight attendant replied
wonderfully, "Yes sir, it means you are never home and have no

life, now sit down and shut up. There are people ahead of you!" It really happened, and people applauded. It was a beautiful sight.

Half of my life is spent on planes, so please pardon another plane story. This one is different, because it happened in Houston. The plane had been pushed back from the gate in Houston, and now we were pulling back in. We anxiously awaited the mechanical problem announcement in our future. Every seat was full, with the exception of the one next to me. I was relaxed and reclined in seat 4A. First class tonight baby, life is good. They re-opened the door, and on walked the most massive indi-

> I think cloning is morally and ethically wrong! Unless of course you could clone a chicken and a centipede...that way everybody could have a drumstick.
> *Mike G. Williams*

vidual I have ever seen. The passengers looked up and began shouting various versions of, "We love you, Hulk." He sat down next to me. I don't even like pro wrestling. I think it's fake. I sat next to *The Undertaker* a few weeks before, and he really needed a shower. Ironically, convenient stores now sell Pro Wrestling Air Fresheners for your car. I'm sorry, but I don't want my *Nissan Frontier* to smell like *The Undertaker*. So now what? What was I going to say to the most famous wrestler the world has ever known? "Hey dude, nice abs, loved that cheesy, low-budget, Blue Thunder thing you did, where did you get that cool bandana?"

I overheard him telling the flight attendant that he was on his way home to see his son, who had just broken his leg at Junior League hockey practice. I would not want to be a certain parent at the next hockey dad's dinner, greeting Mr. Hogan with, "Hi, I'm the father of the boy who put your son out of the game for the whole season. The Mrs. and I are really sorry. I guess the little Hulkster is not as tough as you yet, aye? Ha, ha, ha, could I get an autograph?"

After we got into the air, the pilot used the intercom to ask us all not to bother Mr. Hogan during the flight. Mr. Hogan sat quietly, reading a book entitled *Don't Sweat the Small Stuff.*

A few minutes later, I turned to him and quietly said, " How are you doing tonight, Terry?" *Terry is his real name.* His chiseled chin turned toward mine as he replied in a deeply intimidating voice, "Does *the Hulkster* know

> I'm young at heart, but slightly older in other places.
> *Mike Atkinson*

you?" The Hulkster, like we were talking about someone else not in the room.

"No, the Hulkster doesn't know me, but we have a mutual friend." I'm sure everybody comes up to him and tells him about a mutual friend before asking for an autograph.

"And who might that be who is a *friend of the Hulkster?*"

Right about now I'm thinking he needs to mellow with the third person bit. "It is a guy who used to play in a band with you. You played bass and he played keyboards. The band was called *Naked On Stage.*"

"And who is that and how well do you know him?"

"His name is David White and he played keyboards for me on my last four CD's," I said in a way that would let him know he was sitting next to a celebrity also. *The Mikester* has some pride.

He dropped the Hulk persona and became Terry again. And for the next hour and a half, we talked about life. We talked about our kids and our wives. We talked about our businesses, and even the real

> If I were a Priest, I wouldn't want to be promoted. Because once you become a Bishop, you can only move diagonally.
> *Tim Jones*

story behind the NWO. We talked about David White, who was probably the truest friend he had ever known. He explained how David had become a religious guy, one of those

"Bible Christians;" I believe were his exact words. He began to tell me what a positive influence this *Bible Christian* guy had been to his life. Even though he did not convert to David's faith, he was profoundly moved by his passion for Christ. I pray one day he will be moved all the way to David's faith. I'm thankful for people who let their light shine.

I gave Terry one of my CD's that night and autographed it for his son. Maybe I can pass on a little light to the next wrestling generation through my stupid songs. It *is* what my humor is really all about. Finding a ticklish way to pass along the joy that only God can give. I hope your life is about that, too. I hope you use your talents to light the torch of freedom for the captive in your world. Ironically, later that evening, a beautiful lady turned to me and said, "Your name is Mike Williams, right?" I had a strange urge to say, "Does *the Mikester* know you?" But I didn't. I just sat down on the couch, glad to be home with my beautiful wife again.

**Prayer:** *Father, may I treat with respect and dignity, whomever I meet today. Help me remember that everyone has feelings. They have hurts and pains as I do. Allow me to be a real Bible Christian and influence many with the glorious light of the gospel. Amen.*

*Let your Christian light shine so much that others see the good works and give God the glory.*
Matthew 5:16

# 27

# The Sting of Deodorant Will Never Be Felt Again

*The difference between a nagging wife on the front porch and a barking dog on the front porch, is if you let them both in, the dog will be quiet.*

Killer Beaz

*I*t seems ludicrous to rise before the sun. God never intended for mankind to be awake in the darkness. A squinted glance in the mirror reveals that during the night Grizzly Adams possessed my face. Be forewarned, my breath is now capable of killing small animals. I begin the transformation by stepping into the combination of glass, aluminum, valves, and soap scum. I dial up the necessary temperature and mumble my first prayer of the day. "Our Father, who art in…"

Immediately following the shower comes the customary brushing of the teeth. A brand new high-powered rotary brush does this. It is similar to what you would see at a car wash, only on a smaller scale. After the brushing and spitting comes the flossing. I prefer to use those little pre-strung floss harps with a toothpick on the end. I have large hands, and they don't really fit well in the back of my mouth. Next comes the gargling with Dr. Tichenor's Antiseptic/Mouthwash Concentrated Formula. Four ounces of the juice makes three gallons of mouthwash. In its undiluted form, you can use it to disinfect wounds, sterilize medical utensils, unclog drains, and remove pet stains from upholstery. I gargle with it straight up and undiluted. No sissy, watered-down peppermint oil for me; I'm a real man. I have no enamel adhering to my teeth anymore, but it is a small price to pay for nice breath. This stuff is a speaker's dream. A dash of this stuff before you speak and you will never have to clear your throat again that day. Did I mention that you can also use it as a spot remover? Now a nice shave from my trusty *Bic* single-edge disposable, and I'm ready for the deodorant.

> The Pope rides around in a bulletproof van... C'mon, if he's afraid to die, we're all in trouble.
> *Tim Wilson*

I use a chemical stick deodorant. Hard green jelly, FD&C yellow #6, glycerin, and all of it with the heavy-duty scent of Old Spice. I reach for the container, and I find it bare. It appears that my child has found a new toy and used it all up. There are a few things a man could skip in an emergency. The flossing, the hair conditioner, the foot powder, and the Zit-B-Gone medicated pimple pads, but not the green stuff. Fear not my friends, I'm fully prepared. There is a new sleeve right under the sink. Opening the door, I reached in blindly and grabbed the pit sauce on the first try. I pop the top, and my brain guides my hand toward that soft smooth area of baby skin untouched by the sun. Push hard, and you only have to do one good pass. I love to save time. "OOOOUCH, YANGO, MOMMA, YAAAA!" I forget to remove the little plastic shield of death the company places under the cover. You know the one. This feeble attempt to make a product tamper-proof has ripped a pimple from my armpit. It hurts like a monkey— however a monkey must hurt. My eyes are watering hard, and I am thinking of words that will cause me to need to gargle again if I articulate them. Have you ever done that? Good, I hate to be the only idiot out there with an all-access pass.

Some people might say no pain, no gain. My motto has always been no pain, no pain!

Let us consider some of the things that bring me pain. There is the beautiful glass and iron coffee table my wife leaves in the middle of living room all night long in the dark. Who can forget the 1996 Chevy Corvette convertible matchbox car my son consistently leaves on the floor outside the shower door? I remember a yo-yo that came loose from its string and flew across the room like a pair of Mexican bolos. Can you say three stitches? Some of you have written me bad checks for this book and my bank is charging me ten bucks for your goof up. That pains me. It pains me when I forget I left my soup on the stove until suddenly I smell it burning! *Oh man! Okay, I'm back now.* It has a little burned smoky smell. I will think of it as a mesquite treat! I did not include death in my list because I have not died as of the typing of this book.

> During the Great Depression my grandfather took a job as a dog catcher. He explained that it was so that even if he didn't get a paycheck, he could still eat. Then he just smiled and went back to sleep.
> *Mike G. Williams*

I do know something about death, though. I've seen it. I've watched it take friend and foe alike. I've watched it ravage a village with disease. I've seen it take infants with AIDS. I have seen it murder and kill and destroy students in classrooms around the country. And I've sat by the bedside of a dying saint and seen it creep into the room and I've said, "Thank you."

Thank You, Jesus. There is something amazingly different about the death of a believer. Because for the believer in Christ Jesus, the sting of death has been swallowed up in victory. We do not mourn as those who have no hope. We have an anchor that keeps the soul steadfast and sure though the billows roll. Some may call it a crutch, but I, sir, am a crippled man.

Bill Gaither sang, "There's a room filled with sorrow and sad faces, without hope death has wrapped them in doom, but in another room the saints are rejoicing, for life cannot be sealed in a tomb!" Hallelujah, the sting is gone. We can go to the cemetery this afternoon and wander through those granite monuments of injustice and we can laugh. We can laugh out loud. Paul said, "Death has been swallowed up in victory. Where, O death is your victory? Where, O death is your sting? Thanks be unto God who gives us the victory through the Lord Jesus Christ! Therefore my beloved, be steadfast, immovable, serving hard, because your work is not in vain."

**Prayer:** *Father, I thank You for the promises that allow me to look death in the face and laugh. The many promises that let me know that this world is not it and I'm going to live forever. Help me to live with promise on my lips today. Amen.*

*Where, O death is your victory? Where, O death is your sting? Thanks be to God, who gives us the victory through Jesus Christ.*
1 Corinthians 15:55

# 28

# Don't Worry,
# Be Happy

*"Your platform is national illiteracy. If you met an illiterate person, what would you tell them?"*
*"I would tell them to buy a book."*

A 1997 Miss America contestant

*H*ere's a little song I wrote, I hope you learn it note for note, don't worry, be happy." Now go back and sing it again with a Jamaican accent, *mon*. Whistle it out! Just do it! One thing I like about the island music is that it is never repetitive. Haha! Was that critical? Have you been to the Islands? Growing up in Chicago, going to the Islands meant Blue Island and Rock Island. Neither suburb you would want to vacation in today without fully automatic weapons.

I have the opportunity every year to speak on these religious cruises. I call them *religious* rather than *Christian* because of the sin and degradation that goes on in the name of ministry. I've gotten used to all-night parties, and the disco dancing has not bothered me. I'm used to finding some of the group trying out the slots and their occasional island pina coladas. I am not vexed by the blatant exploitation of Chinese-made Mexican blankets. What really gets my goat, is the sin of gluttony! I believe in moderation in all things, and these boats put me on a soapbox. Or maybe I should say a pizza box. Do we really need appetizers for breakfast? Between the sit-down dinners, they stuff you with buffets and brunches. On my last cruise, a twenty-four-hour pizza bar kept calling me like demons from the pit. "Mr. Williams, you know you want some and we can be at your door in minutes. It's been an entire hour since your last call." *Get thee behind me, Domino's!*

> I'm almost getting better at this!
> *Chapman Clay Williams*

Sometimes they give me the *complimentary* speaker's room that could easily fit on a postcard. We are talking about an Altoids box, with slightly less ventilation. It is so low in the ship that I need a snorkel and mask to get to it. The bathroom is literally so small I have to decide what I'm going to do before I go in, so I'll know whether to pull in or back in. I go stir crazy on these ships. That is especially true if there is more than one day at sea. I got trapped on a miserable tug out of New Orleans one time and thought I would hang myself before we got back. I'm claustrophobic. I don't even like tight shirts. I found myself watching this television show on *great prison escapes* and admiring the size of their rooms. This cruise was felt like Alcatraz with a good catering service.

> It's people like you that make people like me.
> *Lester Moran*

But really, how selfish can I be? I'm here in the Caribbean Islands for one week and I'm already complaining. How American. Let's hold hands and sing a verse of *It's All About*

*Me, Jesus.* Sometimes I ponder what the men and women of history have gone through for the sake of the gospel, and I become ashamed of my pettiness. When I consider the persecuted church in China, I want to crawl under a rock for even voicing my complaints about the pool hours. When I walk past the memorials of the soldiers that have died, some for causes not worth fighting for, I am shaken. When I consider the number of those who have spent their lives hoping for a ship that will never come in, I am silenced. When I open my eyes to the fact that there are prisoners all around me, those who have been imprisoned by fear, doubt, abuse, habits, mental illness, handicap, sickness, disease, and poverty, I am ashamed of myself. All of these and many others that are behind bars that were not necessarily those of their own making. What can I do but offer up praise and thanksgiving for my decrepit little cabin?

> If you hold a seashell to your ear, you can hear the ocean. If you hold a box of Chinese carryout to your ear, you can hear little kitties.
>
> *Mike G. Williams*

The radio plays a simple song that brings me to tears every time I hear it. A moving song from a group named *GLAD*. The music reminds me of the hope that is offered to the unjustly imprisoned of history. Let me loosely interpret their phrases.

*From your dungeon a rumor is stirring about freedom,*
*And you have heard it over and over again,*
*But this time it's your cell key that's turning,*
*And outside you see faces of friends,*
*And though your body is weary and wasted,*
*You begin to feel strong once again,*
*Your prayers have been heard and your ransom,*
*Has been paid in full, be glad.*

You may not be in the depths of despair today, but maybe you can see those depths from your house. Maybe physically you are free to roam the streets and work a job and have children, but inside of you there are dead man's bones. Jesus hurts for you. He is touched by the feelings of your infirmities. He stands outside each of our prison doors with the keys and with the ransom. Let Him free you from your bonds. Open the door and be glad. Be glad that every debt that you ever had has been paid up in full by the grace of God through Jesus Christ our Lord. Be glad.

It is a bit of irony to me that the writer of the *Be Happy* song committed suicide. I guess superficial happiness is not good enough over the long run. So today, remember your freedom and be glad, rejoice in the Lord and shout for joy because you are free.

**Prayer:** *Father, I first ask for You to make Yourself real to those who are unjustly imprisoned around the world by Your adversary. I also ask that You would break through the areas of my life that are still being held prisoner in some way and free me. Forgive me for pettiness. Amen.*

**Be glad in the Lord and rejoice, and shout for joy.**
Psalms 32:11

# 29

# Didn't Even
# Smell Like Smoke

*I would like to get a full body tattoo of me, only thinner.*

Steven Wright

It was a glorious day! I was taking the car out for the first time without parental supervision. Do you remember your first solo flight without a parent in the car? It was like a wave of freedom rushed over your soul and you could breathe again. I can remember that day very well. We were a two-car family at the time. We had a big Chevy touring van with tall-back bucket seats, four speaker stereo, and dual air conditioners. We also had the *other car*. It was a 1969 Ford LTD, blue with a green door. The air conditioner was a non-factory add on. It looked like somebody took a home window a/c and just wedged it up and under the dash. The tunes were brought to you courtesy of one speaker connected to an 8-track player. For a teenager, this car was the *Black Hole of Calcutta* on four wheels.

My friend Ken and I were making a long journey, two miles down the street to the K-Mart store. Some of you people are saying, "Aw, you support K-Mart?" To those people, let me assure you we didn't know about their Walden Book connection at the time. I am taking a stand and will no longer support K-Mart. *I now get all my clothes and paper products at Bob's Drive-Thru Clothing & Liquor Barn.* Anyway, Mom was out in the old car, and Dad finally relinquished the van keys to me. He smiled and said in no uncertain terms, "Don't even scratch it."

I love to drive vans. If you swing the wheel back and forth, right to left to right and so on, the back of the van will bounce side to side. It looks like a rather large choir member trying to get down the aisle and into the choir loft. We had the windows down and the radio blaring. We were waving at girls. It was two fat boys ready to rock and roll. During our little drive, a crazy idea came to mind. *When I get up to the K-Mart entrance, I will turn the wheel and give it a little extra gas and the back end of the van will slide a little on the rain-soaked street.* It was a great idea at the time.

> Always remember that you're special and unique, just like everyone else.
>
> *Justin Fennell*

I entered the turn lane a little fast. I was going about sixty-five when I turned the wheel hard right and gave it some extra gas. Looking back on it, I see now where I might have given it a little too much gas. Well, instead of getting a slight little sway in the back, we got a blender set on puree. We were spinning through the parking lot at sixty-five plus, all the while screaming like the Vienna boys choir with their fingers caught in a door, *which I imagine would sound incredible.* The van came to rest between a car and a light pole as the engine stalled. We sat there shaking and mumbling incoherently.

I clearly remember my thoughts in those brief moments when time stood still as we were swirling around. Volumes can pass before my mind's eye in milliseconds. *Will we live to see another day? What will Dad do to me if I do survive? Should I join the Newsboys? Would a Vera Wang strapless look good on me?* You know, crazy thoughts that roll through your head. Most of all I remember praying a simple prayer that I had prayed often in school. "Dear God, if you will get me out of this one, I will be a missionary and eat monkey meat." I was fluent in that prayer, and if God was listening, I should be in Zimbabwe today.

I suppose the pursuit of happiness seems at times almost as tragic and futile a gesture, as the loading of the ice-making machine onto the Titanic.

*Dennis Miller*

I always wondered what a missionary might pray if he were in a jam. "Dear God, if you get me out of this one, I will go back to America and eat steak for a month." Well, I found a little insight into that question in the story of Shadrach, Meshach, and Abednego. These guys found themselves in a bit of a pickle because they would not bow down and worship a dumb old statue. They appeared before the king, who threatened to *furnace them* for not bowling. Whoops, I meant bowing and I typed bowling. *As if the king was going to say, "You guys better put on the funky multi-colored shoes and bowl!"* Bowing, you know what I mean, bowing. In that day I might have said, "Look here boys, just bow down and humor the king, it's not like you have to mean it." But these three *missionaries* to Babylon said, "NO! You can throw us in the furnace if you want, but our God will deliver us. And even if He doesn't, we will serve Him."

What guts, what strength, what a way to live. Living with nothing to lose and nothing to prove. Totally trusting God and impervious to the outcome. You cannot find where the three boys freaked out and started making deals with God on their way to the furnace. What can you offer God when you have already given everything? Bound hand and foot, they were thrown into the fire. Now, apparently the king liked to sit outside the furnace and watch stuff burn. Seriously, it wasn't like he could go back into the castle and catch a movie on cable. *The only movie made at the time was The Ten Commandments and he wasn't a big fan of it.* His eyes watered as he peered into the blazing furnace. Through the smoke and vapors he saw our three buds accompanied by an angel with asbestos wings. Nebuchadnezzar spouted, "Shadrach, Meshach, and Abednego come out of the fire. Angel baby, you stay put." Here is where the greatest miracle of the entire Bible takes place. It says in Daniel chapter three that when they came out, they didn't even smell like smoke. Wow! Amazing! You are most likely contemplating why I would call that the *numero uno* of supernatural phenomena. Because I can't walk in and out of a convenience store without smelling like smoke! That's why.

Following God has never meant that there would be no problems. In fact, it seems that the closer I follow, the more furnaces I am asked to walk through. But I have learned to trust His leading, from experience.

There is now or will be soon, a time when your life is spinning around you, seemingly out of control. Let me make a few suggestions. First, don't live by the *let's make a deal* plan with God. Serve Him every day and give Him everything you have from the get go. Secondly, trust Him to take care of you. Lastly, remember that you are not alone in your fiery trial. There may just be an angel sitting next to you. I can't believe I said that. It sounds so feminine. Okay, the angel is really massive, works out a lot, and has huge asbestos wings.

**Prayer:** *Father God, creator of all that is or ever shall be, I praise You now. I give You my life, my family, my job, my relationships, my everything. Help me to reject the idols the world offers me every day, even if that will cost me something. Yes, even if that will cost me everything. Amen.*

*The fire had no power over the bodies of these men; their hair was not singed, their clothes were not burned, and they didn't even smell like smoke.*
Daniel 3:27

# 30

# If Pigs Can Fly—
# I Need To Wear
# a Raincoat

*The condition of our world is so backwards... it makes you wish you were dyslexic just so you could have a shot a getting it right somehow.*

Gordon Douglas

*W*e scurried down the narrow jet-way dragging our overloaded carry-on luggage behind us. As I entered the fuselage, I ducked my head ever so slightly to avoid a nasty knot on the noggin. Aircraft may be made of aluminum, but they don't flex as much as one might think. As I entered the bowels of the plane I was hit in the head with a wall of heat. I went from cool and comfortable to *sweating like a pig* in the twinkling of an eye. We are not talking about normal, outside temperature heat; we are talking about *toaster oven* heat... *McDonald's lawsuit coffee heat!* "We have the a/c on. It should cool in just a few minutes," the flight attendant explained. I dropped my computer bag into my seat and headed back out the door. The eighty-degree jet way seemed a welcome oasis from the blazing heat of the cabin. Only a few seconds later, a disgruntled pilot came tearing out of his own sweltering cockpit throne and out the side jet-way door. When the pilot returned from below the plane a few minutes later, he looked at me and said, "Idiots! All of them are Idiots! Some idiot technician connected us to the heater rather than the air conditioning! Those stupid idiots!" I use the word idiot in place of a few other words that he selected for his verbal description. I can't really blame him.

So, the "technician" guy, hooked up the heat instead of the air conditioning on a hot summer day? Was this really the *brain-trust* that I wanted servicing the aircraft that was getting ready to fly thirty-eight thousand feet above the ground at five hundred and fifty miles per hour with me in it? What if he drained the oil, instead of filling it? What if he loosened the wheel lugs rather than tightening them? I'm afraid there were just too many "what if" questions to count. Besides, I had to get to Seattle. This kind of thinking can cause you to get off a plane and have a small but lengthy panic attack! I know!

> Righteousness builds up the people, but sin brings about pain, hardship, and judgment to all that are involved.
> *King Solomon*

Twenty minutes later, with the climate problem corrected, I was finally settled back in my seat for a watching of the safety instruction video. You may have guessed it… they are having trouble with the tape. Who would have thought? They resorted to doing the safety instructional talk verbally. This soliloquy explains about the oxygen masks, the emergency exit row, what to do in the event of a water landing, and how to buckle a seat belt. *I'll tell you right now, with so many things going afoul, if that girl can't connect the seat belts… I am getting off of this airplane!* I love what the

Southwest airline employees say as they explain the oxygen masks, "In the event of a sudden loss of cabin pressure the ceiling above you will open to reveal oxygen masks… STOP-SCREAMING… and place the gold cup over your nose and mouth and try to breathe normally." Then they giggle. But seriously, when it comes to air travel I want to know, or at least believe that everyone is doing their job right. And doing it right the first time! Air conditioning and video tape included! And I don't think that is too much to ask.

When it comes to my life, which entails quite a bit of air travel, doing it right pays off. When it comes to living life itself, which will one day entail some heavenly air travel, doing it right pays off also. Doing it right today, avoids major pitfalls tomorrow. Just as with air travel, apathy on the job could cost us our lives or the lives of our children. So it is with the path God has set before us. I would like to *suggest*, or rather *implore you*, to follow the instructions for life from the Author of life. Jesus Christ laid out the plan and the maintenance schedule for an eternal "flight," and it behooves us to follow the instructions to the letter. Do it right and never become apathetic!

I understand that it is not easy to *follow hard* after God. It goes against our very nature. We are always looking for an easy way out. Sometimes we like to become lazy in the name of Grace. *I will discuss that concept in another book that I am currently working on in my spare time.* Following God has been one of the toughest callings of my life. But it's a calling that is worth *fighting hard* for. Maybe it hasn't been that way for you… maybe we are following different gods. *Wow, that was kind of harsh… sorry.* Though the yoke may be easy and the burden may be light… there is still a yoke and a burden involved. Do it right. Look into the scriptures and find out how to live like Jesus. If He is to be our example, let's read how he did it, and do that. And I know that God will equip you through His Spirit to be victorious in Him. Fight hard – fight on – victory is in sight! I'll see you in the next book or I will see you on the other side. Either way is okay with me.

*My friends, carefully build yourself up in this most holy faith, pray in the Holy Spirit, stay in the center of God's love, keep your arms and outstretched, ready for the mercy of our Master, Jesus Christ. This is the value filled life! Be gentle with those who are slower in the faith and chase those who wander astray. Be compassionate, but never soft on sin. Salutations now to Him who can keep you standing on your righteous feet until you enter His presence! Salutations to our one God, our Savior and Master Jesus Christ, be glory, majesty, power and rule, now and forever. Amen!*

Jude 1:20-25